Alive in Christ

GRADE 2

Sacraments of Penance and Eucharist

aliveinchrist.osv.com

The Subcommittee on the Catechism, United States Conference of Catholic Bishops, has found this catechetical series, copyright 2014, to be in conformity with the *Catechism of the Catholic Church*.

Nihil Obstat
Rev. Fr. Jeremiah L. Payne, S.Th.L.
Censor Librorum, Diocese of Orlando

Imprimatur
✠ Most Rev. John Noonan
Bishop of Orlando
March 26, 2013

© Our Sunday Visitor

Contents at a Glance

THE CHURCH YEAR Feasts and Seasons **9**

UNIT 1: Revelation **52**
Chapter 1: God's Gifts **53**
Chapter 2: God's Promise **63**
Chapter 3: The Word of God **73**

UNIT 2: Trinity **86**
Chapter 4: God the Father **87**
Chapter 5: God the Son **97**
Chapter 6: God the Holy Spirit **107**

UNIT 3: Jesus Christ **120**
Chapter 7: God's Commandments **121**
Chapter 8: Choose to Do Good **131**
Chapter 9: God's Mercy **141**

UNIT 4: The Church **154**
Chapter 10: The Sacraments **155**
Chapter 11: Seek Forgiveness **165**
Chapter 12: The Church Year **175**

UNIT 5: Morality **188**
Chapter 13: Welcome in the Kingdom **189**
Chapter 14: Share the Good News **199**
Chapter 15: Ways to Pray **209**

UNIT 6: Sacraments **222**
Chapter 16: Gather to Worship **223**
Chapter 17: Listen to God's Word **233**
Chapter 18: Remembering Jesus' Sacrifice **243**

UNIT 7: Kingdom of God **256**
Chapter 19: Supper of the Lamb **257**
Chapter 20: Go Forth! **267**
Chapter 21: A Feast for Everyone **277**

CATHOLIC SOCIAL TEACHING Live Your Faith **290**

OUR CATHOLIC TRADITION Faith Basics **304**

Contents in Detail

Opening Lesson 1

Welcome to Alive in Christ, Grade 2. This chapter introduces you to the different parts of your book and invites you to learn, love, and celebrate your Catholic faith.

God's Word Children of God Galatians 3:26–27

The Church Year Feasts and Seasons 9

In these lessons, you learn about special days and times of the Church year that celebrate Jesus and honor Mary and the Saints.

Ordinary Time

Mother of Mercy 9

God's Word Wedding at Cana John 2:1–5

Called to Be Saints 15

God's Word Image of His Son Romans 8:28–29

Advent

Change Our Hearts 19

God's Word Change Your Hearts Mark 1:1–8

Christmas

Glory to God 25

God's Word God Chose You Ephesians 1:3–6

Lent

Teach Me Your Ways 31

God's Word God Made Us for Good Works Ephesians 2:10

Easter

The Three Days 37

God's Word Innocent Luke 23:46–48

We Rejoice 43

God's Word Peace Be with You John 20:19–21

Pentecost 47

God's Word Filled with the Holy Spirit

Acts of the Apostles 2:1–4

iv

UNIT 1: **Revelation** — 52

Chapter 1: **God's Gifts** — 53

God's Word Handing Down the Stories Luke 1:1-2
The Creator and Humans Psalms 8:2, 7–9

- God is the Creator of all that is good.
- Jesus is God's greatest gift. Jesus is the Son of God.

Chapter 2: **God's Promise** — 63

God's Word The Sinner Who Repents Luke 15:7 The Garden of Eden Genesis 2:15–17; 3:1–6, 23 The Good Shepherd John 10:11–14

- God sent his beloved Son, Jesus, to bring all people back into his friendship.
- Jesus is the Savior and the Good Shepherd.

Chapter 3: **The Word of God** — 73

God's Word Jesus Among the Crowds Luke 6:17–18
The Great Flood Genesis 6–9 Jesus Teaches and Heals Matthew 4:23–25

- God tells his People about himself through the Bible.
- The Bible is God's Word written by humans.

Unit 1 Review — 83

UNIT 2: **Trinity** — 86

Chapter 4: **God the Father** — 87

God's Word Trust in the Father Luke 12:29-31 Rely on God
Matthew 6:25-32

- God is our Father who created us and cares for us.
- We can trust in God because he loves us.

Chapter 5: **God the Son** — 97

God's Word My Beloved Son Luke 3:21–22 Announcing Jesus' Birth Luke 1:26–38; 2:1–11 The Boy Jesus in the Temple Luke 2:41–52 Baptism of Jesus Matthew 3:13–17

- Jesus is the beloved Son of God born of Mary.
- Jesus is the Savior of the world who showed us God the Father's love.

Chapter 6: **God the Holy Spirit** — 107

God's Word Risen Jesus Appears to Disciples Luke 24:49
The Promise John 14:15–26 The Spirit Comes Acts 1:4–5, 8; 2:2–3

- The Holy Spirit guides the Church and helps you to be a disciple.
- The Holy Trinity is one God in three Divine Persons.

Unit 2 Review — 117

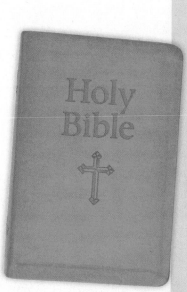

UNIT 3: Jesus Christ — 120

Chapter 7: God's Commandments 121

🔹 **God's Word** Moses on the Mountain Exodus 24:12 Love the Lord Your God Luke 10:27 The Parable of the Good Samaritan Luke 10:29–37

- The Ten Commandments are God's laws to his People.
- Jesus teaches you to love God above all things and love others as you love yourself.

Chapter 8: Choose to Do Good 131

🔹 **God's Word** Peter Hears the Rooster Mark 14:69–72 Peter Denies Jesus John 18:17–18, 25–27

- Conscience is the ability given to us by God that helps us make choices about right and wrong.
- Sin is a free choice to do what you know is wrong.

Chapter 9: God's Mercy 141

🔹 **God's Word** Forgive Seventy-Seven Times Matthew 18:21–22 The Prodigal Son Luke 15:11–32

- God is merciful and forgiving.
- God will always forgive you if you are truly sorry.

Unit 3 Review 151

UNIT 4: The Church — 154

Chapter 10: The Sacraments 155

🔹 **God's Word** Jesus Heals a Blind Man Luke 18:35–43 The Commissioning of the Apostles Matthew 28:19–20

- Grace is a share in God's life and help.
- Sacraments are special signs and celebrations that come from Jesus and give grace.

Chapter 11: Seek Forgiveness 165

🔹 **God's Word** Whose Sins You Forgive John 20:21, 23 The Woman Who Was Forgiven Luke 7:36–39, 44–50

- In the Sacrament of Penance and Reconciliation, you receive God's forgiveness.
- This Sacrament also celebrates your friendship with God and the Church.

Chapter 12: The Church Year 175

🔹 **God's Word** The Holy Family Celebrates Passover Luke 2:41–42

- The Church year celebrates the life, Death, Resurrection and Ascension of Jesus.
- The Resurrection is the mystery of Jesus being raised from the dead.

Unit 4 Review 185

UNIT 5: Morality — 188

Chapter 13: Welcome in the Kingdom 189

God's Word Let the Children Come Luke 18:15–17 Zacchaeus the Tax Collector Luke 19:1–10 Blessing of the Children Matthew 19:13–15

- The Kingdom of God is the world of love, peace, and justice that is in Heaven and is still being built on Earth.
- Everyone is welcome in God's Kingdom and in the Catholic Church.

Chapter 14: Share the Good News 199

God's Word Jesus' Disciples Receive a Mission Mark 16:15–16 The Vine and the Branches John 15:4–5

- Jesus' disciples share in his life and in his work.
- The Holy Spirit helps us proclaim the Gospel in our words and actions.

Chapter 15: Ways to Pray 209

God's Word The Lord's Prayer Luke 11:1–4 How to Pray Matthew 6:5–9

- Prayer is being with God in your mind and heart. We pray in many ways, for many reasons.
- Jesus taught his followers the Lord's Prayer.

Unit 5 Review 219

UNIT 6: Sacraments — 222

Chapter 16: Gather to Worship 223

God's Word The Road to Emmaus Luke 24:30–32 The Community Gathers Acts 2:42–47

- Mass is another name for the celebration of the Eucharist.
- The assembly uses songs, prayers, and actions to worship God.

Chapter 17: Listen to God's Word 233

God's Word The Parable of the Yeast Luke 13:18–21 The Mustard Seed Matthew 13:31–32

- In the Liturgy of the Word, God's living Word is read.
- We profess what we believe about God and pray for the needs of the Church and the world.

Chapter 18: Remembering Jesus' Sacrifice 243

God's Word Give God His Due Matthew 6:24 The Rich Young Man Matthew 19:21–22

- The Eucharist is a memorial of the sacrifice Jesus made.
- The Liturgy of the Eucharist is the second main part of the Mass.

Unit 6 Review 253

UNIT 7: **Kingdom of God** **256**

Chapter 19: Supper of the Lamb **257**

🔲 **God's Word** The Bread of Life John 6:30–35
The Feeding of Five Thousand Luke 9:10–17

• Through the Eucharist, Jesus' followers are united with him and one another.
• The gift of Holy Communion is received with reverence.

Chapter 20: Go Forth! **267**

🔲 **God's Word** Paul Proclaims the Kingdom Acts 28:30–31
Peter Preaches Acts 10:42–48

• The Church's mission is to share Jesus' love and to profess the Good News of the Kingdom of God.
• All members of the Church share in her mission.

Chapter 21: A Feast for Everyone **277**

🔲 **God's Word** Jesus Knocks Revelation 3:20 The Wedding Feast
Matthew 22:2–10 and Luke 14:16–23

• Heaven is the full joy of living with God forever.
• The Eucharist is a sign of joy and of what Heaven will be like.

Unit 7 Review **287**

Catholic Social Teaching Live Your Faith . . . **290**
These pages introduce you to important teachings of Jesus and the Church that help us live Jesus' New Commandment to love as he loved.

Life and Dignity **290**
Call to Community **292**
Rights and Responsibilities **294**
Option for the Poor **296**
The Dignity of Work **298**
Human Solidarity **300**
Care for Creation **302**

Our Catholic Tradition Faith Basics **304**
This reference section presents information on our Creeds, Sacraments, morality, prayers, and practices of our Catholic faith.

We Believe **304**
We Worship **307**
We Live **318**
We Pray **320**

Catholic Faith Words **328**

Index **332**

A New Year

 Let Us Pray

Leader: Loving God, you share your Word with us in the Bible. Thank you for inviting us to be your children.

> "Enter, let us bow down in worship;
> let us kneel before the LORD who made
> us." **Psalm 95:6**

All: Thank you, God, for sharing your life and love with us. We want to listen to your Word and live in your love.

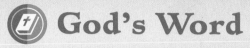 **God's Word**

"For through faith you are all children of God in Christ Jesus. For all of you who were baptized into Christ have clothed yourselves with Christ."

Galatians 3:26-27

? What Do You Wonder?

- What does it mean to be God's children?
- How does God invite us to know and love him?

Second Grade

What's going to happen this year?

This year is all about learning, loving, and celebrating our Catholic faith!

When you see 📖, you know it's a story or reading from the Bible. Through Bible stories you will discover that Jesus the Son shares God's love and mercy.

When you see ♥, you know it's time to pray. Each time you are gathered together, you can listen to and talk to God in prayer. You will grow closer to Jesus as you pray and get to know his teachings.

When you see ▶, you will sing songs to praise God and celebrate our faith. You'll explore the Church's feasts and seasons and meet many Saints, our heroes of the Church.

Underline two things you will do this year.

The gold star above begins an exercise to help you learn what's being taught. You may underline, circle, write, match, or draw.

Special Signs and Celebrations

A big part of this year is learning about the **Seven Sacraments**. The Sacraments are special signs and celebrations that Jesus gave his Church. Important words like this are **highlighted** in yellow so you don't miss them.

You'll discover how the Church celebrates God's love and forgiveness in the Sacrament of Reconciliation. You will explore the different parts of the Mass and learn how Jesus gives himself to us in the Eucharist.

Everything you learn and do in class will help you take part in parish celebrations in new ways.

Catholic Faith Words

In this box you will see the **highlighted** words again and their definitions.

Seven Sacraments special signs and celebrations that Jesus gave his Church. They allow us to share in God's life and work.

Share Your Faith

When you see these fun green words, you know it's time for an activity!

Think What is something you know about Church celebrations?

Share Talk in a small group about how you learned this. Write one new thing you learned from your group.

_____

_____

God's Word

Where can you find stories about God?

The **Bible** is the Word of God written down by humans. It is one great book, made up of many small books. In fact, the word Bible means "books." The books of the Bible are divided into two parts: The Old Testament and the New Testament.

Another name for the Bible is Scripture, which means "writing." We hear readings from Scripture during Mass and the other Sacraments.

Catholic Faith Words

Bible the Word of God written down by humans

⭐ Circle the names of the people you have heard of.

The Old Testament
The first part of the Bible and also the largest. It tells about God and his love for us, especially the Jewish people, before Jesus was born.

Noah   Moses   Esther

The New Testament
The second part of the Bible tells of God's love for people after the coming of Jesus. It is about the life and teaching of Jesus, his followers, and the early Church.

Mary   Jesus   John the Baptist

The Gospels

The New Testament begins with four very special books called Gospels. The word Gospel means, "Good News." These four books of the Gospels tell of the Good News Jesus brought of the Kingdom of God and his saving love.

- The Gospel according to Matthew

- The Gospel according to Mark

- The Gospel according to Luke

- The Gospel according to John

The Gospels are filled with stories about Jesus, the words of Jesus, words other people said about Jesus, and stories that Jesus told.

Connect Your Faith

📖 God's Word

"Go into the whole world and proclaim the gospel to every creature." Mark 16:15–16

Word

Verses

Chapter Number

Book Name

Find the Bible Passage

Find the Bible passage in Chapter 7, page 123 and write the book name, the chapter number, and the verse.

Book Name: _____

Chapter: _____

Verse: _____

Our Catholic Life

What does it mean to be Catholic?

Each chapter in your book has an Our Catholic Life section. This section shows you in a special way what it means to be Catholic. Words, pictures, and activities help us grow closer to Jesus and the Church.

Grow as a Follower of Jesus

- know more about our faith
- understand and take part in the Sacraments
- live as Jesus calls us to
- talk and listen to God in prayer
- be an active member of the Church
- help others know Jesus through our words and actions

People of Faith

Look for this box, where you will meet People of Faith, holy men and women who loved God very much and did his work on Earth.

Live Your Faith

Be a Person of Faith! Draw yourself in the picture frame.

Tell how you can be a Person of Faith this year.

♥ Let Us Pray

Pray Together

Every chapter has a prayer page, with lots of different ways to pray. You may listen to God's Word read from the Bible, pray for the needs of others, call on the Saints to pray for us, and praise God the Father, Son, and Holy Spirit in words and songs.

Gather and begin with the Sign of the Cross.

Leader: Blessed be God.

All: Blessed be God forever.

Leader: Let us pray.

Bow your heads as the leader prays.

All: Amen.

Leader: A reading from the holy Gospel according to John.

Read John 6:35–38.

The Gospel of the Lord.

All: Praise to you, Lord Jesus Christ.

 Sing "Alive in Christ"

We are Alive in Christ
We are Alive in Christ
He came to set us free
We are Alive in Christ
We are Alive in Christ
He gave his life for me
We are Alive in Christ
We are Alive in Christ

© 2013, John Burland. All rights reserved.

FAMILY+FAITH
LIVING AND LEARNING TOGETHER

YOUR CHILD LEARNED >>>

This page is for you, the parent, to encourage you to talk about your faith and see the many ways you already live your faith in daily family life.

God's Word

In this section, you will find a Scripture citation and a summary of what your child has learned in the chapter.

Catholics Believe

- Bulleted information highlights the main points of doctrine of in the chapter.

Here you will find chapter connections to the *Catechism of the Catholic Church.*

People of Faith

Here you meet the Saint, Blessed, or Venerable featured in People of Faith.

CHILDREN AT THIS AGE >>>

This feature gives you a sense of how your child, at this particular age, will likely be able to understand what is being taught. It suggests ways you can help your child better understand, live, and love their faith.

How They Understand the Lessons Your second-grader has begun to understand that he or she is not the only person in the world. He or she can learn to see things from perspectives other than their own which means they are beginning to develop empathy and compassion.

At age seven or eight most children are capable of making moral choices. You can help your child develop morally by giving them good examples and clear moral guidelines. With that your child will be able to choose between right and wrong.

At this age children love to celebrate. Many like music and find comfort in ritual. Try singing some hymns at home with them and using gestures when you pray as a family. Don't hesitate to do spontaneous prayer with your child or to have them lead family prayer.

CONSIDER THIS >>>

This section includes a question that invites you to reflect on your own experience and consider how the Church speaks to you on your own faith journey.

LET'S TALK >>>

- Here you will find some practical questions that prompt discussion about the lesson's content, faith sharing, and connections with your family life.

- Ask your child to share one thing they've learned about their book.

LET'S PRAY >>>

This section encourages family prayer connected to the example of our People of Faith.

Holy men and women, pray for us. Amen.

For a multimedia glossary of Catholic Faith Words, Sunday readings, seasonal and Saint resources, and chapter activities go to **aliveinchrist.osv.com**.

Mother of Mercy

 Let Us Pray

Leader: Mother of Mercy, pray for us that we show kindness and mercy when it is needed.

The LORD is kind and merciful.

Based on Psalm 103

All: Amen.

 **God's Word**

Mary was at a wedding feast in Cana. Jesus and his friends were there too. Mary saw that there was no more wine for the guests. She told Jesus, "They have no wine." Jesus asked his mother how this affected him. His time had not yet come. But Mary turned to the servants and said, "Do whatever he tells you."

Based on John 2:1–5

? What Do You Wonder?

- What would have happened if the food or drinks had run out?
- Why did Mary want to help?

9

Ordinary Time

Ordinary Time occurs twice in the year. The Church celebrates the words and works of Jesus.

In Ordinary Time the priest wears green. The church is decorated in green, too.

There are many feasts of Mary during Ordinary Time. The Church color for Mary's feasts is white.

Mary's Example

Mary is the Mother of Jesus. She is the greatest of Saints. The Church honors Mary with different titles. One of these titles is Mary, Our Lady of Mercy—to show mercy means to be forgiving and loving to others. Mary is an example of love, kindness, and forgiveness.

Ordinary Time

- This season of the Church year comes twice, after Christmas and for a longer time after Easter.

- During this time, we learn more about Jesus' teachings so we continue to grow as his disciples.

- We also honor Mary and the Saints.

Mary is the Mother of God and our Mother, too. She loves us and welcomes us with open arms.

Acting Out of Love

Mary's actions showed love. She stayed with her cousin Elizabeth who was going to have a baby. She searched for her Son, Jesus, when he was lost in Jerusalem. Mary stayed at the Cross when Jesus died. She forgave those who hurt him, as Jesus did. Mary shows us how to love and forgive others.

Showing Mercy

Merciful people think of what others need and try to help. God is merciful. He forgives us when we sin. Jesus shows us how to be merciful, too. Many of his stories in the Gospels are about being merciful.

➡ How has Jesus shown his mercy to us?

➡ How has someone shown mercy to you? How can you show mercy to others?

Underline the way that Mary showed mercy to others after Jesus' Death.

Activity

Act Out a Mercy Prayer Make gestures to go with this mercy prayer. Show what the words mean. Say the mercy prayer every morning.

Jesus, have mercy on me.
Mary, help me show mercy to others today. Amen.

People of Faith

Chapter	Person	Feast Day
1	Mary, Mother of God	January 1
2	Saint Cristóbal Magallanes Jara	May 21
3	Saint Luke	October 18
4	Julian of Norwich	May 13
5	Saint Peter	June 29
6	Saint Arnold Janssen	January 15
7	Saint Elizabeth of Hungary	November 17
8	Saint Thérèse of Lisieux	October 1
9	Saint Jane Frances de Chantal	August 12
10	Saint Pius X (Giuseppo Sarto)	August 21
11	Saint Benedict-Joseph Labré	April 16
12	Pope Saint Victor	July 28
13	Saint Brigid of Kildare	February 1
14	Saint Teresa of Calcutta	September 5
15	Saint Alphonsus Liguori	August 1
16	Saint Tarcisius	August 15
17	Saint Paul	June 29
18	Blessed Imelda Lambertini	May 13
19	Venerable Pierre Toussaint	
20	Saint Anthony Claret	October 24
21	Saint Mary Magdalene de Pazzi	May 25

Mary

Saint Peter

Pierre Toussaint

♡ **Let Us Pray**

Hail Mary

Gather and begin with the Sign of the Cross.

Leader: A reading from the holy Gospel according to Luke.

Read Luke 1:39–42, 45.

The Gospel of the Lord.

All: Praise to you, Lord Jesus Christ.

Bow your heads and pray the Hail Mary together.

Side 1: Hail, Mary, full of grace, the Lord is with thee. Blessed art thou among women and blessed is the fruit of thy womb, Jesus.

Side 2: Holy Mary, Mother of God, pray for us sinners, now and at the hour of our death. Amen.

Leader: Go forth to love and serve the Lord, as Mary did throughout her life.

All: Thanks be to God.

 Sing "Mary, Our Mother"

Mother of Jesus, be with us every day.
We want to stay close to you always.
You are our mother.
We are your children.
Guide us in every way each day.
Guide us in every way.

© 1998, John Burland. All rights reserved.

FAMILY+FAITH
LIVING AND LEARNING TOGETHER

TALKING ABOUT ORDINARY TIME >>>

Feasts of Mary and the Saints occur all during the Church Year. Ordinary Time is the longest of all the Church seasons. It has thirty-three or thirty-four Sundays. It is called Ordinary Time because all the Sundays are numbered in order. Ordinary Time is divided into two parts. The first is from the end of the Christmas season until Ash Wednesday. The second is from the end of the Easter season until the first Sunday of Advent, which begins the next cycle, or a new liturgical year.

God's Word

Read **John 2:1–11**, the Gospel story of the Wedding Feast of Cana. It is the first miracle or sign in the Gospel according to John. It also helps us think about Mary's compassion for others and her trust in Jesus.

HELPING YOUR CHILD UNDERSTAND >>>

Mercy

- Most children this age understand mercy as being given another chance. They need to be encouraged to expand that understanding to include forgiveness.

- Usually at this age, children need some guidance to understand that as a follower of Jesus, they need to offer others mercy and forgiveness.

- For the most part, children learn the concept of mercy from receiving mercy. They need to trust that when they make mistakes, they are still loved.

CATHOLIC FAMILY CUSTOMS >>>

Mercy and Forgiveness

Each time a family member gives another an overt sign of forgiveness, or the benefit of the doubt, or minimizes negative responses to honest mistakes, he or she extends mercy to the other. When acting in these ways, you are giving your child an experience of, or an example of, God's (much greater) capacity for mercy and forgiveness.

FAMILY PRAYER >>>

Say this prayer together sometime during the month of October.

Mary, our Mother and model of Mercy, teach us to be merciful and kind to each other. We pray that you will ask God to show his mercy to all who are in need of it. We ask this in Jesus' name. Amen.

For a multimedia glossary of Catholic Faith Words, Sunday readings, seasonal and Saint resources, and chapter activities go to **aliveinchrist.osv.com**.

Called to Be Saints

 Let Us Pray

Leader: Dear Jesus, you are always with me. You help me to be a child of the light. You guide me to make right choices. Thank you.

"The LORD is my shepherd;
   there is nothing I lack." Psalm 23:1

All: Amen.

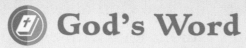 **God's Word**

We know that for those who love God, all things work together for good. Those whom God created were made in the image of his Son, in order that he might be the first born within a large family.

Based on Romans 8:28–29

? What Do You Wonder?

- In what ways are you like Jesus?
- How does Jesus care for you?

15

Remembering Our Saints

The Feast of All Saints, on November 1, honors all people who are in Heaven. We do not know the names of all those who are in Heaven. But the Church sets aside this day to celebrate everyone enjoying God's presence forever.

We know that Baptism makes a person a member of the Church. Everyone who is baptized shares a mission to be children of the light.

This means you love God above all things and that you share his love with everyone. It also means you share the Good News of Jesus.

God calls you to do your mission for your whole life. When someone who has lived like a child of the light dies in God's grace, that person joins God in Heaven forever. We are happy for all those in Heaven. We call them Saints.

Many of the Saints are our relatives who lived before us. The Church honors these Saints on All Saints Day. On that day, we remember that we want to be like them. The Saints care about us. They will pray with us and for us if we ask them to.

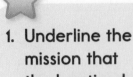

1. Underline the mission that the baptized members of the Church share.

2. Circle what it means.

© Our Sunday Visitor

♥ Let Us Pray

Giving Thanks

Gather and begin with the Sign of the Cross.

Leader: Let us pray.
Lord God, you bless us with the gift of life.

All: We give you thanks.

Leader: You gave us all the gifts of creation.

All: We give you thanks.

Leader: You made us your children, your holy People.

All: We give you thanks.

Leader: You invite us to love you by loving others.

All: We give you thanks.

Leader: You have given us your Spirit.

All: We give you thanks.

Leader: Dear God,
You have given us everything.
We bless your name.
We thank you.

▶ **All:** Sing "Litany of Saints"

Pray for us. Pray with us.
Help us to share God's love.

© 1991, John Schiavone. Published by OCP. All rights reserved.

17

FAMILY+FAITH
LIVING AND LEARNING TOGETHER

TALKING ABOUT ORDINARY TIME >>>

On the Feast of All Saints, we honor all the Saints—the holy men and women in Heaven who are examples for us. We also call to mind that each of us is called in Baptism to be a holy person, a person guided by the light of Christ. For Catholics, All Saints' Day is a holy day of obligation.

God's Word

Read **Romans 8: 28–29**, one of Paul's last letters where he speaks strongly about faith and the transforming power of Baptism.

HELPING YOUR CHILD UNDERSTAND >>>
Saints

- Most children this age wonder about Heaven and what it is like.
- At this age many children like to have a patron Saint.
- In most cases children are beginning to understand the connection between their relationship with God and the choices they make in their lives.

FEASTS OF THE SEASON >>>
All Saints' Day
November 1

This is a wonderful time to highlight the good qualities of family members who have passed away. If your child shares a spiritual quality with a family member, point it out in a compliment, such as, "You are like your great-grandma, who was always generous and outspoken for justice." Although we cannot know with certainty who is in Heaven, encourage your child to view departed relatives as spiritual allies in the Communion of Saints.

FAMILY PRAYER >>>

Use this prayer to pray for all family members who have passed away in recent years:

Dear Jesus, we are children of the light on Earth. We know that there are children of the light in Heaven. We pray that our relative (name) is living happily with you today. With all of the Saints, we honor you, your Father, and the Holy Spirit. Amen.

For a multimedia glossary of Catholic Faith Words, Sunday readings, seasonal and Saint resources, and chapter activities go to **aliveinchrist.osv.com**.

Change Our Hearts

 Let Us Pray

Leader: Lord, God, send your Holy Spirit
to help us see your path more clearly.

"...prepare the way of the LORD!" Isaiah 40:3

Through Christ, our Lord.

All: Amen.

 **God's Word**

The Jewish people were waiting for the Messiah to come. Many had turned away from God. John the Baptist said to them, "Turn back to God. Be sorry for your sins. Change your hearts." Based on Mark 1:1–8

? What Do You Wonder?

- What does it means to change your heart?

- What words or actions tell someone that you are sorry?

Preparing

Advent is the first season of the Church year. During the four weeks of Advent, the whole Church prepares to celebrate Jesus' coming again in glory.

Purple is the Advent color. The priest wears purple colors. The church has purple decorations.

The color purple reminds you to change your heart for Jesus' Second Coming. It reminds you to ask for God's forgiveness and mercy.

Advent

- The season of four weeks before Christmas.

- During this time, we prepare to celebrate the coming of Jesus.

Using a purple marker or crayon, underline what we prepare for during Advent.

Las Posadas is a celebration in Mexico that honors Mary and Joseph's journey to Bethlehem before Jesus' birth.

Closer to God

Sometimes you may forget that God is near. You may make choices that draw you away from God. Advent is a good time to remember God's love for you. It is a time to draw closer to him.

➤ **What is one way you would like to grow closer to Jesus during Advent?**

Activity

Fill the Manger Inside the manger, write one way you will show your love for others during Advent. Decorate the manger to make a soft bed for Baby Jesus.

Prayer for God's Mercy

This is a prayer of petition. A prayer of petition is an asking prayer. In this prayer we ask for God's mercy and forgiveness.

 Let Us Pray

Gather and begin with the Sign of the Cross.

Leader: Our help is in the name of the Lord.

All: Who made Heaven and Earth.

Leader: Lord, you came to gather all peoples in peace. Lord, have mercy.

All: Lord, have mercy.

Leader: Lord, you came to show us how to be holy. Christ, have mercy.

All: Christ, have mercy.

Leader: Lord, you will come again in glory to save your people. Lord, have mercy.

All: Lord, have mercy.

Leader: May God have mercy on us, forgive us our sins, and bring us to everlasting life.

All: Amen.

Listen to God's Word

Leader: A reading from the holy Gospel according to Mark.

Read Mark 1:14–15.

The Gospel of the Lord.

All: Praise to you, Lord Jesus Christ.

Pray Around the Advent Wreath

Sit in silence before the Advent wreath. Think of a way you will change your heart during Advent.

Leader: Glory be to the Father, and to the Son, and to the Holy Spirit:

All: as it was in the beginning, is now, and ever shall be, world without end. Amen.

Go Forth!

Leader: Let us go forth to love and serve the Lord by showing kindness to one another.

All: Thanks be to God.

 Sing "Candles of Advent"

FAMILY+FAITH
LIVING AND LEARNING TOGETHER

TALKING ABOUT ADVENT >>>

The word Advent means coming. Advent is the season when the Church prepares to celebrate the coming of Jesus, the Savior, into the world and reminds us that he will come again on the last day. During this time, we prepare ourselves for the joy of Christmas and for the Second Coming of Christ. For centuries, the People of Israel in the Old Testament waited in great hope for the coming of a Messiah. Despite their great desire for a Messiah, many often failed to prepare their hearts for his coming. The centuries of waiting for the Messiah muted their anticipation. John the Baptist was sent as a messenger to exhort the people to repent and ask forgiveness. Each Advent, we hear this same call in a special way.

God's Word

Read **Mark 1:1–8**, John the Baptist challenges his hearers to repent and ask forgiveness in preparation for receiving the Messiah.

HELPING YOUR CHILD UNDERSTAND >>>
Advent

- Most second-graders are preparing to celebrate the Sacrament of Reconciliation for the first time this year. They need help from you to understand that sorrow for sin includes a willingness to change habits, attitudes, and actions that keep them from loving God, others, and self.

- Most younger children will not fully grasp the reality of the Second Coming of Christ. It is more helpful for them when you emphasize sorrow for sin and change of behavior as one of the ways we get ourselves ready for the joy of Christmas.

FEASTS OF THE SEASON >>>

Las Posadas
December 16–
December 24

Las Posadas (Spanish for "the inn") is a traditional Mexican ritual that takes place from December 16 through December 24. It is, in essence, a novena. Families re-enact the moment when Joseph and his pregnant wife, Mary, search for a room as her time to give birth approaches. Children and adults join in procession to different homes every night asking for lodging for the night. People are invited in to read Scriptures, pray, and sing Advent songs and Christmas carols called villancicos. A fiesta begins, and refreshments are provided by the hosts.

FAMILY PRAYER >>>

Have family members share one thing they did to prepare their hearts for Jesus' coming during the day. Then pray:

God, the Father of mercies, you willed your Son to become a man in order to give life back to us. Bless this food, your gift, so that with new strength, we may prepare for the glorious coming of Christ. Amen.

For a multimedia glossary of Catholic Faith Words, Sunday readings, seasonal and Saint resources, and chapter activities go to **aliveinchrist.osv.com**.

Glory to God

♡ Let Us Pray

Leader: Dear God, we are so happy you sent us your Son, Jesus. Thank you. We want to be as loving and kind as he was. We want to give you glory.

"May God be gracious to us and bless us; may his face shine upon us." **Psalm 67:2**

All: Amen.

📖 God's Word

Blessed be the God and Father of our Lord Jesus Christ, who has blessed you in Christ with every blessing. God chose you before the world was created. He wants you to be holy and loving. He adopted you as his children through Jesus Christ. God wants you to give him glory. **Based on Ephesians 1:3–6**

❓ What Do You Wonder?

- What kind of blessings does God give you?
- How do children give glory to God?

25

Season of Christmas

Christmas is a joyful season. It lasts from the Feast of Christmas on December 25 until the Feast of the Baptism of Jesus. During this season, the priest wears white or gold vestments. You can see the Christmas Nativity scene in church for the whole season. You'll also hear about all the things that happened to Jesus as a young child.

Underline the best gift God has given to the world.

Glory to God

The Church celebrates the birth of Jesus at Christmas. We remember that Jesus is the best gift God gave to the world. God sent an angel to tell some men who watch sheep (shepherds) that Jesus the Savior was born. The angel told them to go to a stable to find him. Then the angels sang a song of praise to God.

Share the Good News

The angel shared the Good News about Jesus with the shepherds. At Mass, we sing what the angels sang that first Christmas:

Glory to God in the highest,
and on earth peace to people
of good will.   Based on Luke 2:8–14

Like us, the shepherds in the fields were people of faith. They believed what the angel told them about Jesus. After they saw the Baby Jesus, they shared the Good News with others.

➜ **What other Good News about Jesus do you know? Who can you tell?**

Activity

Welcome Baby Jesus
Draw how your family welcomes Jesus at Christmas.

27

Celebrate Christmas

This prayer is a celebration of the Word and an act of praise and thanksgiving. It is a moment of prayer with the Church, using the Scriptures.

 Let Us Pray

Gather and begin with the Sign of the Cross.

Leader: Blessed be the name of the Lord.

All: Now and forever.

Leader: Let us pray.

Bow your heads as the leader prays.

All: Amen.

Listen to God's Word

Leader: A reading from the holy Gospel according to Luke.

Read Luke 2:8–14.

The Gospel of the Lord

All: Praise to you, Lord Jesus Christ.

Come forward and pray before the Nativity scene.

Leader: God, our Father, we thank you for the gift of Jesus, your Son.

All: We praise you, we bless you, we thank you.

Leader: We thank you for all the gifts of creation.

All: We praise you, we bless you, we thank you.

Leader: We ask your blessing on all your people.

All: We praise you, we bless you, we thank you.

Go Forth!

Leader: Go forth to sing of God's glory and to share his peace with others.

All: Thanks be to God.

 Sing "Away in a Manger"

Away in a manger, no crib for a bed,
the little Lord Jesus laid down his sweet head.
The stars in the sky looked down where he lay,
the little Lord Jesus, asleep on the hay.

Be near me, Lord Jesus, I ask thee to stay
close by me forever, and love me I pray.
Bless all the dear children in thy tender care,
and take us to Heaven to live with thee there.

Away in a manger, no crib for a bed,
the little Lord Jesus, asleep on the hay.

Verse 1, Little Children's Book for Schools and Families, ca. 1885; verse 3,
Gabriel's Vineyard Songs, 1892, alt. Music: William James Kirkpatrick, alt.

FAMILY+FAITH
LIVING AND LEARNING TOGETHER

TALKING ABOUT CHRISTMAS >>>

The Christmas season begins with the celebration of Christ's birth on December 25 and ends with the Feast of the Baptism of the Lord. During this time, the Church celebrates all of the events of Jesus' early years until he begins his public ministry at his baptism. The liturgical color of the season is white or gold. All of the Christmas liturgies during this season are joy-filled. They celebrate the arrival of the Messiah, and they send the assembly forth to spread the Good News of the light of Christ found in the People of God.

God's Word

Read **Ephesians 1:3–6** to learn about Paul's image of God's unlimited love that includes all as members of the same body who work together to spread the Gospel.

HELPING YOUR CHILD UNDERSTAND >>>
Christmas

- Most children this age are fascinated by the story of the birth of Jesus, and they love to visit the parish Nativity scene. Take time to go to the Nativity scene several times during the Christmas season.
- Ordinarily, second-graders know some popular Christmas hymns; repetition of those hymns teaches them the story and the meaning of the season.

CATHOLIC FAMILY CUSTOMS >>>
Christmas Traditions

Catholic family rituals and traditions are important for faith development for the whole family. They lend deeper meaning to adults and give children a stable base to grow on. You are probably passing on some of the traditions of your childhood. If you have not started any yet, consider some of these:

- Read the Christmas story from the Gospels every Christmas Eve or Day as your family gathers to open gifts.
- Bless your house on the feast of the Epiphany. You can find directions and prayers at **aliveinchrist.osv.com**.
- Donate new and used clothes, toys, books, or games to a thrift store or shelter.
- Teach your child a Christmas hymn (Silent Night, Joy to the World). Sing it often. The repetition will help them remember the words.

FAMILY PRAYER >>>

God, our Gracious Father, we give you thanks and praise for all the blessings and gifts you have given us, especially the gift of your Son, Jesus. Amen.

For a multimedia glossary of Catholic Faith Words, Sunday readings, seasonal and Saint resources, and chapter activities go to **aliveinchrist.osv.com**.

Teach Me Your Ways

 Let Us Pray

Leader: Lord, God, send your Holy Spirit
to guide our actions and make them loving.

"Let the words of my mouth be acceptable,
the thoughts of my heart before you."
Psalm 19:15a

Through Christ, our Lord.

All: Amen.

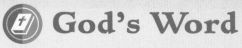 **God's Word**

We are the work of God's hands, created in Jesus Christ. God made us to lead a life of good works.

Based on Ephesians 2:10

What Do You Wonder?

- What does God's handiwork look like?

- What kinds of good works can children do?

Love and Sacrifice

Lent is a season to change our hearts. It begins on Ash Wednesday, and it lasts forty days. The priest wears purple during Lent, and the church is decorated in purple.

The forty days of Lent are a good time to think about God's loving kindness to all people. When the people had turned from God, he sent them a Savior. No matter how many times we sin, God still invites us back into friendship with him.

Each day during Lent, the whole Church reads and listens to stories of God's love. We hear the stories of the works of Jesus. We hear about his sacrifice to save us from our sins. As we listen, we try to think of ways that we can be more loving to others.

Underline the things that the Church does during Lent.

32 The Church Year

Love God and Others

You are learning many stories about Jesus. As you learn these stories, you will find new ways to follow him. Jesus teaches us to remember one very important thing: Love God above all things, and love your neighbor as you love yourself.

➜ **What is one way you could love your neighbor as much as you love yourself?**

Activity

Unscramble the Message Unscramble the words to find one very important thing Jesus teaches us.

OLVE OGD
VELO RUYO
GBEHRONI

☐☐☐☐ ☐☐☐,
☐☐☐ ☐☐☐☐
☐☐☐☐☐☐☐☐

Celebrate Lent

This prayer includes a signing prayer. A signing prayer is a ritual prayer of action where the Sign of the Cross is traced on your body.

 Let Us Pray

Gather and begin with the Sign of the Cross.

Leader: O Lord, open my lips.

All: That my mouth shall praise you.

Leader: Lord Jesus, you have shown us the way to the Father.

All: Lord, have mercy.

Leader: Lord Jesus, you have given us the truth.

All: Christ, have mercy.

Leader: Lord Jesus, you lead us to everlasting life.

All: Lord, have mercy.

Leader: May almighty God have mercy on us, forgive us our sins, and bring us to everlasting life.

All: Amen.

Listen to God's Word

Leader: A reading from the holy Gospel according to John.

Read John 3:16–17.

The Gospel of the Lord.

All: Praise to you, Lord Jesus Christ.

Signing of the Senses

Leader: Let us pray. Father of our Lord, Jesus Christ, you chose us as your holy people.

Trace a cross on your forehead.

Leader: Jesus shared the Good News with others.

Trace a cross on your lips.

Leader: Jesus, you showed us how to love by forgiving and healing others.

Trace a cross on your heart.

Go Forth!

Leader: Father, your Son Jesus teaches us your ways. Help us to know, love, and serve you, now and forever. In Jesus' name we pray.

All: Amen.

 Sing "These Ashes"

These ashes we receive reminding us
it's time for a change of heart.
These ashes we receive reminding us
it's time for a brand new start,
to follow in Jesus' way, to follow in Jesus' way.

35

FAMILY+FAITH
LIVING AND LEARNING TOGETHER

TALKING ABOUT LENT >>>

Lent is a forty-day journey that begins on Ash Wednesday. The receiving of ashes on one's forehead marks a promise to repent or change to grow closer to God and the Church. It is also a reminder for families to work on strengthening their relationships. Reconciliation between siblings, sacrificing for one another, and praying together as a family are all ways the Lenten journey can bring conversion to your home.

God's Word

 Read **Ephesians 2:10**, and reflect on the idea of you personally being God's handiwork.

HELPING YOUR CHILD UNDERSTAND >>>

Lent

- Usually at this age, children are able to name some of the things they can change to grow closer to Jesus.
- Most children this age can relate to the concept of conversion through the Gospel stories of Zacchaeus and the Prodigal Son.
- Children at this age ordinarily need some concrete ideas and modeling on how to change behavior.

FEASTS OF THE SEASON >>>

Feast of Saint Joseph
March 19

Saint Joseph is the foster father of Jesus. He was a man of faith and obedient to God. He loved and protected his wife, Mary, and provided for his family. Many parishes celebrate the feast with a Saint Joseph's Table where people can enjoy a meal and buy homemade baked goods. The proceeds usually go to the poor.

FAMILY PRAYER >>>

 During Lent, pray this prayer often before your family meals:

Leader: May God, our merciful Father, grant you all the joy of returning, like the Prodigal Son, to the happiness of this house.

All: Amen.

Leader: May Christ guide you through your journey of Lent to change your heart.

All: Amen.

Leader: May Almighty God bless us, the Father, the Son, and the Holy Spirit.

All: Amen.

For a multimedia glossary of Catholic Faith Words, Sunday readings, seasonal and Saint resources, and chapter activities go to **aliveinchrist.osv.com**.

The Three Days

❤ Let Us Pray

Leader: Lord, God, you are always taking care of us.
Even when we forget, you are there.
Help us to remember your love.
Through Christ, our Lord.

"But I trust in you, LORD;
I say, 'You are my God.'
My destiny is in your hands."   Psalm 31:15–16a

All: Amen.

📖 God's Word

"Jesus cried out in a loud voice, 'Father, into your hands I commend my spirit'; and when he had said this he breathed his last. The centurion who witnessed what had happened glorified God and said, 'This man was innocent beyond doubt.' When all the people who had gathered for this spectacle saw what had happened, they returned home beating their breasts."

Luke 23:46–48

❓ What Do You Wonder?

- Why did Jesus die?
- Why did the people let Jesus die?

We Remember

The Church sets aside a whole week to remember Jesus' dying and rising. It is called Holy Week. It begins on Passion Sunday and ends on the evening of Easter Sunday. The first days are part of Lent. On Palm Sunday, the people welcomed Jesus with the words,

"Hosanna to the Son of David!" Matthew 21:9

There are three very special days in Holy Week. These days are called the Easter Triduum.

- Holy Thursday

- Good Friday

- Holy Saturday

Circle the three special days during Holy Week.

Members of the assembly carry the Cross during a procession on Good Friday.

Good Friday

On Good Friday, the Church remembers the day that Jesus died on a Cross. He died to save all people from sin and everlasting death. On this day, people walk up in a procession to honor the holy Cross. They bow or kneel before the Cross. Sometimes they touch or kiss it. They do this to thank Jesus for giving his life for us.

Helping Others

Jesus carried his Cross to the place where he would die. He loved all people so much he was willing to die for them. When we do something that is difficult in order to help others, sometimes we say that we are "carrying a cross," too. We are willing to think of their needs.

➜ **What is something you have done for others, even though it was hard?**

Activity

Make a Cross Decorate the cross. Think of a time when you had to do something difficult. Touch the cross and say a prayer. Ask Jesus to help you, and he will!

Honor the Cross

This celebration includes a Prayer of the Faithful, which is a prayer of intercession. We also pray a ritual prayer of honoring the Cross.

 Let Us Pray

Gather and begin with the Sign of the Cross.

Leader: O Lord, open my lips.

All: That my mouth shall speak your praise.

Bow your heads as the leader prays.

Leader: Let us pray.

All: Amen.

Prayer of the Faithful

Leader: Let us pray for the holy People of God.

All: Lord, guide your Church.

Leader: Let us pray for our bishop, for all bishops, priests, and deacons, and for all who work in ministry in our Church.

All: Holy Spirit, guide our leaders.

Leader: Let us pray for all in our parish who are preparing for Baptism.

All: Lord, make them members of your family.

Procession to the Cross

Fold your hands and pray silently to Jesus. Walk up slowly and in silence to honor the Cross. Bow deeply and touch the foot of the Cross.

All: Sing "We Remember (The Three Days)"

We remember; we give thanks.
We remember.
God's love is everlasting.
All thanks and praise to God.

Go Forth!

Leader: We believe that by his dying
Christ destroyed death forever.
May he give us everlasting life.

All: Amen.

Leader: May almighty God bless us,
the Father, the Son, and the Holy Spirit.

All: Amen.

FAMILY+FAITH
LIVING AND LEARNING TOGETHER

TALKING ABOUT EASTER >>>

Holy Week is the holiest week of the Church Year. It begins on Passion Sunday and continues until Evening Prayer on Easter Sunday. The Triduum or "three days" mark the most sacred time of Holy Week. It begins at sundown on Holy Thursday and ends at sundown on Easter Sunday. During these three days, the whole Church fasts and prays with anticipation and hope. On Good Friday, the assembly participates in the Adoration of the Cross. The Church prays special prayers for the salvation of the world at Good Friday services, and the full Passion is read. No hosts are consecrated on Good Friday; the congregation receives hosts that were consecrated at the Holy Thursday evening Mass.

God's Word

Read **Luke 23:1–49**, the story of Jesus' Passion and Death on the Cross.

HELPING YOUR CHILD UNDERSTAND >>>

Holy Week

- Usually children this age are interested in the events of Holy Week.
- Most children in second grade have either recently received First Communion or are preparing to do so. Participation in Holy Thursday services would benefit them.
- Ordinarily, children this age find it difficult to understand why Jesus died if he was innocent.

CATHOLIC FAMILY CUSTOMS >>>

Holy Objects

Throughout Holy Week, talk with your child about the meaning of each day. Teach your child reverence for the holy objects associated with each day.

Bring home palm leaves that are distributed during Passion Sunday Mass. Position them in a place of honor behind a crucifix or religious picture.

On Good Friday, allow your child to reverently hold a cross or crucifix.

FAMILY PRAYER >>>

On Holy Thursday and Good Friday, pray this prayer before your evening meal:

Lord Jesus Christ, who, in fulfilling your Father's will, became obedient unto death; may our spiritual food be like yours: always to do the Father's good and gracious will. For you live and reign forever and ever. Amen.

For a multimedia glossary of Catholic Faith Words, Sunday readings, seasonal and Saint resources, and chapter activities go to **aliveinchrist.osv.com**.

We Rejoice

♥ Let Us Pray

Leader: Lord, God, send your Holy Spirit,
that we will see and hear the Risen Christ
as he guides us to right and loving actions.

"Make known to me your ways, LORD;
teach me your paths." Psalm 25:4

Through Christ, our Lord.

All: Amen.

📖 God's Word

On Easter Sunday evening, the disciples were together in a house. They had the doors locked because they were afraid of the Jews. All of a sudden, Jesus came and stood among them and said, "Peace be with you." He showed them his hands and his side and the disciples rejoiced. Jesus said to them again, "Peace be with you. As the Father has sent me, so I send you."

Based on John 20:19–21

? What Do You Wonder?

- Why were the disciples so afraid?
- How do we experience Jesus' peace in our lives?

A Joyful Season

The whole Church joyfully celebrates the Resurrection of the Lord. The priest wears white vestments. We celebrate Easter for fifty days.

Easter is always in the spring in the northern half of the world. It is the most joyful season in the Church year. We sing Alleluia and ring bells.

After God the Father raised Jesus to new life, Jesus met with his followers several times. They were so happy to see him again! Then Jesus returned to his Father in Heaven. But he promised to send the Holy Spirit to be with them always.

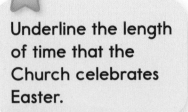

Underline the length of time that the Church celebrates Easter.

Many parishes include an Easter egg hunt for children during the celebration of Easter Sunday.

© Our Sunday Visitor

❤️ **Let Us Pray**

Celebrate Easter

Gather and begin with the Sign of the Cross.

Leader: Light and peace in Jesus Christ, Alleluia.

All: Thanks be to God, Alleluia.

The Lord's Prayer and Peace

Leader: Let us pray in the words that Jesus taught us.

All: Our Father . . .

Leader: May the God of light and peace fill our hearts and lives.

All: Amen.

Leader: Let us offer to each other a sign of the peace of Christ.

Offer one another a sign of peace.

Leader: Go in peace, Alleluia.

All: Thanks be to God, Alleluia.

▶️ Sing "Easter Alleluia"

FAMILY+FAITH
LIVING AND LEARNING TOGETHER

TALKING ABOUT EASTER >>>

The celebration of the Easter season includes the fifty days following the Triduum. The Easter liturgies reflect the joy of salvation. The Alleluia is sung once again. The People of God renew their baptismal commitment in the sprinkling rite. The Gospels unpack the meaning of the Easter event and help the assembly to celebrate God's saving power. We are sent out from the Easter celebration to spread the Good News.

God's Word

Read **John 20:19–21**, the story of two appearances of the Risen Christ to the disciples. The first, when Thomas was absent, and the second, when Thomas was present and expressed his faith.

HELPING YOUR CHILD UNDERSTAND >>>
Easter

- At this age, usually children will enter into the meaning of the season through the songs and the Easter Gospel readings throughout the season.

- Most children at this age can identify with the fear of the disciples, both that the disciples fear the Jews and Jesus' response to their desertion during his Passion.

- Normally, reasoning abilities begin to become more developed at this age, so children may begin to ask more questions about the Easter events.

FEASTS OF THE SEASON >>>

Ascension Thursday

marks the Ascension of the Risen Christ to Heaven, which is celebrated forty days after Easter. It is a holy day of obligation. Sometimes dioceses move the celebration of the feast to the Sunday following Ascension Thursday, the Seventh Sunday of Easter.

FAMILY PRAYER >>>

Joyfully pray this prayer at mealtime on the Sundays of the Easter season:

O God, source of life, fill our hearts with the joys of Easter. In your goodness, you have given us food to eat; grant also that we may continue to live that new life which the Risen Christ has won for us, for he lives and reigns with you forever and ever. Amen.

For a multimedia glossary of Catholic Faith Words, Sunday readings, seasonal and Saint resources, and chapter activities go to **aliveinchrist.osv.com**.

Pentecost

 Let Us Pray

Leader: Come Holy Spirit,
come in power and light to show us
how to live for God alone.

"May the glory of the LORD endure
forever;
may the LORD be glad in his works!"
Psalm 104:31

All: Amen.

God's Word

When the day of Pentecost had come, they were all together in one place. And suddenly from Heaven there came a sound like the rush of a violent wind, and it filled the entire house where they were sitting. Divided tongues, as of fire, appeared among them, and a tongue rested on each of them. All of them were filled with the Holy Spirit and began to speak in other languages, as the Spirit gave them ability.

Based on Acts of the Apostles 2:1–4

? What Do You Wonder?

- What would it have been like to be in the room with the disciples?
- Why do you think they began to speak in other languages?

The Power of the Spirit

The Holy Spirit came to the followers of Jesus on Pentecost, fifty days after Easter. They were gathered in a room together. They missed Jesus. Jesus had gone to be with his Father in Heaven. They were not sure what to do.

Then the Holy Spirit came in wind and fire. Jesus' followers were filled with joy and hope. They went out of the room and began to tell the Good News of Jesus.

Everyone understood their words, and many were baptized that day.

Activity

Write the Gifts Answer the questions to remember Pentecost.

How did the Holy Spirit come to Jesus' followers?

_____

_____

What were Jesus' followers filled with when the Holy Spirit came to them?

_____

_____

Let Us Pray

Celebrate the Spirit

Gather and begin with the Sign of the Cross.

All: Sing "Come to Us, Holy Spirit"

Come to us Holy Spirit
So we can know God's love
Come to us Holy Spirit
So we can know God's love

© 2010, Chet A. Chambers. All rights reserved.

Pray the Sign of the Cross together and bow your heads as the leader prays.

Leader: May the Lord bless us and keep us.

All: Amen.

Leader: May the Lord's face shine upon us.

All: Amen.

Leader: May the Lord look upon us with kindness, and give us peace.

All: Thanks be to God, Alleluia, Alleluia.

49

FAMILY + FAITH
LIVING AND LEARNING TOGETHER

TALKING ABOUT EASTER >>>

The Church celebrates the coming of the Holy Spirit on the Feast of Pentecost. Pentecost occurs fifty days after Easter. It marks the end of the Easter season. On Pentecost, the sanctuary colors and priest's vestments are red, symbolizing the fire of Pentecost and the empowerment of the Holy Spirit.

The images of wind and fire at Pentecost signify the manifestation of God's presence and power. This presence and power transformed the disciples into courageous preachers and teachers who spread the Good News everywhere they went.

God's Word

Read **Acts of the Apostles 2:1–11**, the story of the first Pentecost.

HELPING YOUR CHILD UNDERSTAND >>>

Pentecost

- Children at this age will usually relate very well to the drama of the Pentecost event.
- Ordinarily, children of this age will understand the Holy Spirit as being very powerful.
- Children this age will learn to pray to the Holy Spirit for help when they hear that others do.

FEASTS OF THE SEASON >>>

Feast of Saint Catherine of Siena
April 29

Saint Catherine of Siena is one of four women Saints considered to be doctors of the Church. Saint Catherine once said: "If you are what you should be, you will set the whole world ablaze!"

FAMILY PRAYER >>>

During the week between Pentecost Sunday and Trinity Sunday, pray the following prayer together as an evening prayer:

Come Holy Spirit, set our hearts on fire with love and courage. Guide us to reach out in love to others and to preach the message of Jesus in our actions. Amen.

 For a multimedia glossary of Catholic Faith Words, Sunday readings, seasonal and Saint resources, and chapter activities go to **aliveinchrist.osv.com**.

Units at a Glance

UNIT 1: Revelation 52
Chapter 1: God's Gift. 53
Chapter 2: God's Promise 63
Chapter 3: The Word of God 73

UNIT 2: Trinity 86
Chapter 4: God the Father 87
Chapter 5: God the Son 97
Chapter 6: God the Holy Spirit 107

UNIT 3: Jesus Christ 120
Chapter 7: God's Commandments 121
Chapter 8: Choose to Do Good 131
Chapter 9: God's Mercy 141

UNIT 4: The Church 154
Chapter 10: The Sacraments. 155
Chapter 11: Seek Forgiveness 165
Chapter 12: The Church Year 175

UNIT 5: Morality 188
Chapter 13: Welcome in the Kingdom 189
Chapter 14: Share the Good News 199
Chapter 15: Ways to Pray 209

UNIT 6: Sacraments 222
Chapter 16: Gather to Worship 223
Chapter 17: Listen to God's Word 233
Chapter 18: Remembering Jesus' Sacrifice. 243

UNIT 7: Kingdom of God 256
Chapter 19: Supper of the Lamb 257
Chapter 20: Go Forth! 267
Chapter 21: A Feast for Everyone. 277

Revelation

Our Catholic Tradition

- God gave us many gifts. His gifts tell us about what he is like. (CCC, 41)

- We can learn about God's gifts and his love from the Bible. (CCC, 105)

- Adam and Eve turned away from God. God continued to love them anyway. (CCC, 410)

- Jesus, God's only Son, is God's greatest gift. He is our Savior. He brings us back into friendship with God the Father. (CCC, 430, 452)

How does Jesus help us find our way to God his Father?

Learning more about God through his gifts of creation.

© Our Sunday Visitor

God's Gifts

 ## Let Us Pray

Leader: God, we thank you for all that you have made.

The earth and all that is in it belong to God;
the world and all who live in it are God's.

Based on Psalm 24:1

All: Thank you, God, for creating each of us.
Amen.

God's Word

Many have worked to write about the events that have happened among us just as those who were there at the beginning have handed the events and stories down to us.

Based on Luke 1:1–2

What Do You Wonder?

- What stories do we have about Jesus and his family?
- How do stories teach us to care for the things God has given us?

Praise and Thanks

What is most special about God's creation?

David was a shepherd a very long time ago. He became a king of God's People. He wrote poems of praise and thanks and prayers to God. Many of David's poems are part of the Bible. They are called **psalms**. Sometimes you hear the psalms at Mass.

David often watched the sheep in the fields at night. He was amazed by the wonders of the night sky. As he looked at everything in **creation**, he praised God for his gifts.

David was grateful, most of all, that people had been made in God's own image. This means people can think and love and make choices. Nothing else God made can do these things.

Underline the things that make people different from the rest of God's creatures.

© Our Sunday Visitor

In God's Image

Humans are the most special part of God's creation. God wants you to take care of the many gifts of creation. Here is one of David's psalms about humans.

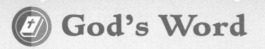

God's Word

The Creator and Humans

"O LORD, our Lord, how awesome is your name through all the earth!... You have given [man] rule over the works of your hands, put all things at his feet: All sheep and oxen, even the beasts of the field, the birds of the air, the fish of the sea, and whatever swims the paths of the seas." Psalm 8:2, 7–9

Share Your Faith

Think Write or draw one way you take care of creation.

Share Talk with a partner about these things.

The Son of God

Why is Jesus God's greatest gift?

David knew that God is the Creator of everything that is good. But David was born too soon to know about God's greatest gift.

God's greatest gift is his Son, Jesus. Jesus is man and God, human and divine. He was human, just like all of us, except in one way. He never disobeyed God the Father. Jesus did not commit **sin**.

Jesus learned about his Jewish faith and how to pray from his family. He listened to Mary, his Mother, and Joseph, his foster father. Jesus did what they asked him to do.

➡ **What are some other things that Jesus might have done that you also do?**

Catholic Faith Words

sin a person's choice to disobey God on purpose and do what he or she knows is wrong. Accidents and mistakes are not sins.

Son of God a name for Jesus that tells you God is his Father. The Son of God is the Second Divine Person of the Holy Trinity.

© Our Sunday Visitor

Alike But Different

While he was on Earth, Jesus saw interesting things every day, just as you do. He enjoyed the flowers, the birds of the air, and the fruit trees. He learned to do new things, just like you.

Jesus is human. He is also divine, which means he is God. Jesus is the **Son of God** who became man. That is why you look to Jesus to learn more about God his Father.

➤ **In what ways are you and Jesus alike? How are you different?**

Connect Your Faith

Find the Hidden Word Color the X's red. Color the O's blue, green, or yellow to find a name for Jesus that you have heard.

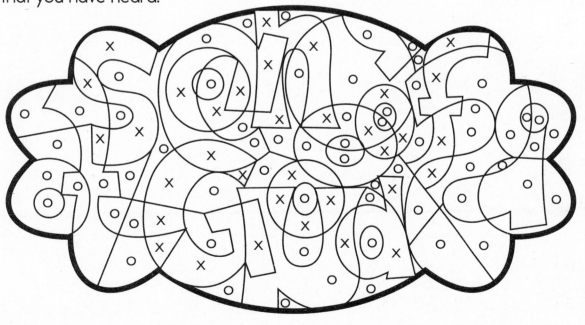

Our Catholic Life

How do people use what God has created?

God created everything from nothing. He shared with us the ability to make things to use and enjoy.

Fill in the blanks with things that can be made from the gifts of God's creation.

Making Use of God's Gifts

Gift of Creation	Things We Make From It
wood from trees	houses, paper, _____
cotton	clothing, _____
wheat	bread, cereal, _____
wool from sheep	sweaters, coats, _____
cacao beans	cocoa, _____

People of Faith

Blessed Virgin Mary, first century

Mary was a special gift from God. God chose Mary to be the Mother of Jesus, his Son. When the Angel Gabriel told her she would be the Mother of Jesus, he said, "Blessed are you!" Mary is also the Mother of the Church. That means that she is our Mother, too. The Hail Mary is the most well known prayer about the Mother of God. We pray the Hail Mary when we pray the Rosary.

January 1

Discuss: What can Mary help you do today?

 Learn more about Mary at **aliveinchrist.osv.com**

Live Your Faith

Tell What gift of God's creation do you see in the picture? How do we take care of this gift of creation?

_____

_____

_____

Write the name of one person or thing that you can take care of.

_____

God's Gifts **59**

♥ **Let Us Pray**

Blessing Prayer

Gather and begin with the
Sign of the Cross.

Leader: Bless God

All: Oh, God, bless

Leader: The wonderful Earth where we live and play.

All: Bless God

Leader: The sun and moon that light our way.

All: Bless God

Leader: The trees and plants both large and small.

All: Bless God

Leader: The birds that fly, the fish in the sea.

All: Bless God

Leader: The people just like you and me.

All: Bless God

Leader: The gift of Jesus, your own Son.

All: Bless God

Leader: Sent to bless us, everyone.

 All: Sing "God Is a Part of My Life"

God is a part of my life.
God is a part of my life.
God is a part of my life;
I rejoice, I rejoice, I rejoice.

© 1995, Carey Landry. Published by OCP. All rights reserved.

© Our Sunday Visitor

FAMILY + FAITH
LIVING AND LEARNING TOGETHER

YOUR CHILD LEARNED >>>

This chapter is about God's gift of creation and the special place humans have in it because we are made in the image and likeness of God.

God's Word

 Read **Luke 1:1–2** to learn more about those who have worked to tell God's story.

Catholics Believe

• God is the Creator of all that is good.

• Jesus is God's greatest gift. Jesus is the Son of God.

To learn more, go to the *Catechism of the Catholic Church* #256, 319, and 454 at **usccb.org**.

People of Faith

This week, your child met the Blessed Virgin Mary who we honor as the Mother of God and the Mother of the Church.

CHILDREN AT THIS AGE >>>

How They Understand God's Creation Most second-graders have a strong sense of cause and effect. This makes it natural for them to believe in a Creator when they see the created world. They also have a strong sense that everything has a purpose. For this reason, it is an excellent time for them to learn that everything in the natural world is a gift from God and has a God-given role or meaning.

CONSIDER THIS >>>

When was the last time that God's creation amazed you?

Do you realize creation is one of the many ways God shows himself to you? God… "is living and personal, profoundly close to us in creating and sustaining us. Though he is totally other, hidden, glorious, and wondrous, he communicates himself to us…in Jesus Christ, whom we meet in the Church, especially in Scripture and the Sacraments. In these many ways, God speaks to our hearts where we may welcome his loving presence" (*USCCA, p. 51*).

LET'S TALK >>>

• Ask your child to talk about God's gifts. Which is his greatest? (Jesus)

• Talk about ways your family uses God's gifts of creation in your daily routines.

LET'S PRAY >>>

Mary, Mother of God, pray for our family and help us always love your Son, Jesus. Amen.

For a multimedia glossary of Catholic Faith Words, Sunday readings, seasonal and Saint resources, and chapter activities go to **aliveinchrist.osv.com**.

Chapter 1 Review

 A **Work with Words** Write the correct words from the Word Bank to complete each sentence.

1. All that God has made is called

   _____.

2. You can _____
   for creation.

3. Jesus did not _____.

4. David wrote _____
   of praise and thanks to God.

5. Jesus is God's greatest _____.

B **Check Understanding** Draw a line from the words ending in Column A to the best ending in Column B.

Column A	Column B
6. Jesus is human and	God is the Father of Jesus.
7. The name Son of God tells you that	Mary and Joseph.
8. God created everything from	Creator.
9. David knew that God is the	the Son of God.
10. Jesus learned how to pray from	nothing.

© Our Sunday Visitor

 Go to **aliveinchrist.osv.com** for an interactive review.

God's Promise

♡ Let Us Pray

Leader: God, we thank you for showing us how to live.

God chose his servant David.
He took David from the sheepfolds.
From tending sheep, God brought him
to shepherd Jacob and his People, Israel.
Based on Psalm 78:70–71

All: Thank you, Father, for sending faithful people
to help us know the way. Amen.

📖 God's Word

Jesus said, "I tell you, in just the same way there will be more joy in heaven over one sinner who repents than over ninety-nine righteous people who have no need of repentance." Luke 15:7

❓ What Do You Wonder?

- How do you talk to God?
- When are some times that you say you are sorry?

Our first parents, called Adam and Eve, in the Garden of Eden.

Free to Choose

What choice did Adam and Eve make?

God gives all people the freedom and ability to choose. The first book of the Bible tells a story about a choice made by Adam and Eve.

📖 God's Word

The Garden of Eden

God put Adam and Eve in a garden called Eden. They had all they needed to live and be happy.

God told Adam and Eve that they were free to eat from all the trees in the garden, except one. God said, "When you eat from that tree, you will surely die."

Satan, a fallen angel and enemy of God and his People, disguised himself as a serpent and said to the woman, "This is not true. If you eat that fruit you will be like God."

Eve saw the tree's fruit and ate some. She gave some to Adam. He ate it, too.

Adam and Eve chose to do what they knew God did not want them to do. So God sent them away from the Garden of Eden.

Based on Genesis 2:15–17; 3:1–6, 23

Catholic Faith Words

Original Sin the first sin committed by Adam and Eve and passed down to everyone

God gave Adam and Eve a choice. Instead of doing what he asked them to do, they chose to disobey God. This is called **Original Sin**.

➔ **What happened to Adam and Eve when they chose to disobey God?**

Share Your Faith

Think Write or draw one way you can obey God at school and one way you can obey God at home.

Share Talk about your response with a partner.

God Sends a Savior

How does Jesus save and lead us?

God did not turn away from Adam and Eve. Instead, God promised to send a **Savior**. God promised that the Savior would lead all people back to friendship with him.

God kept his promise. He sent his own Son to be the Savior of all people. Jesus came into the world to save all people and lead them to God. Jesus wanted people to love God and to be happy with God again.

Catholic Faith Words

Savior a title for Jesus, who was sent into the world to save all people lost through sin and to lead them back to God the Father

© Our Sunday Visitor

66

Jesus, the Good Shepherd

Jesus wanted the people to understand he is the Savior. Jesus told a story to show that he is like a shepherd and his followers are like sheep. Shepherds care for their sheep and lead them to grass and water. Shepherds make sure their sheep do not get lost.

Underline what shepherds do. Talk about how Jesus is like a shepherd.

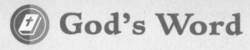 God's Word

The Good Shepherd

Jesus said, "I am the good shepherd. A good shepherd lays down his life for the sheep. A hired man, who is not a shepherd and whose sheep are not his own, sees a wolf coming and leaves the sheep and runs away, and the wolf catches and scatters them…he…has no concern for the sheep. I am the good shepherd, and I know mine and mine know me." John 10:11–14

Connect Your Faith

Another Name for Jesus Fill in the blanks to spell out a title for Jesus.

I am the G ☐ ☐ d S ☐ ☐ p ☐ ☐ r ☐ .

Our Catholic Life

What happens when you make a choice?

You were created in God's image. God gave you the freedom to make choices. You are responsible for the choices you make.

Every time you make a choice, things happen. All choices have results, or consequences. Good choices have good consequences for you and for others. Bad choices can have bad consequences for you and may hurt others.

 Draw a line from the bad choice on the left to the good choice on the right.

Bad Choices	Good Choices
Goofing off at school and not doing your homework	Taking care of your belongings
Making fun of others	Working hard and paying attention in class
Skipping your chores or letting someone else do them	Praying every day
Being careless with what you have been given	Helping out at home without being asked
Not taking time to talk to God	Treating all people with kindness

People of Faith

Saint Cristóbal Magallanes Jara, 1869–1927

Saint Cristóbal Magallanes Jara grew up in Mexico. When he was a boy, he was a shepherd. Later, as a priest, he tried to be like Jesus, the Good Shepherd. He took care of the people in his village by building schools, starting a newspaper, and training men to become priests. He was arrested on his way to say Mass at a farm. Some people thought that he was trying to rebel against the government. He wasn't, but he was killed anyway. Before he died, Saint Cristóbal forgave the people who killed him.

May 21

Discuss: How was Saint Cristobal like Jesus?

 Learn more about Saint Cristóbal at **aliveinchrist.osv.com**

Live Your Faith

Circle Good Actions
Circle the actions that lead to God.

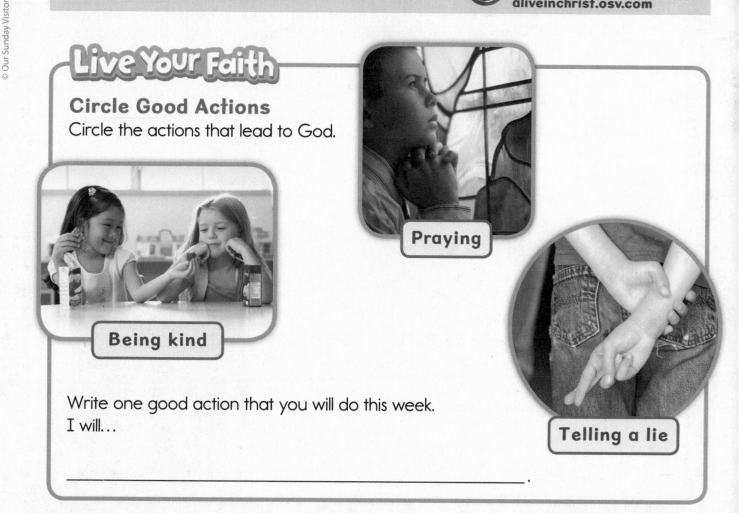

Praying

Being kind

Telling a lie

Write one good action that you will do this week. I will…

_____.

Let Us Pray

Prayer of Praise

Gather and begin with the Sign of the Cross.

Leader: The Lord is my shepherd.
I have all that I need.

All: The Lord is my shepherd.
I have all that I need.

Leader: You lead me to green pastures.
You guide me on the right path.

All: The Lord is my shepherd.
I have all that I need.

Leader: I am not afraid.
Your rod and staff give me courage.

All: The Lord is my shepherd.
I have all that I need.

Leader: Your goodness and kindness follow me
all the days of my life.

All: The Lord is my shepherd.
I have all that I need.
Based on Psalm 23

 Sing "Jesus, Shepherd"
You are the shepherd,
we are the sheep.
Come, Good Shepherd,
lead us home.
Based on John 10: Text and Music © 1990, OCP.
All rights reserved.

FAMILY+FAITH
LIVING AND LEARNING TOGETHER

YOUR CHILD LEARNED >>>

This chapter introduces our need for Jesus, our Savior, who shows us the way to his Father.

God's Word

Read **Luke 15:7** to see how God rejoices when people turn to him.

Catholics Believe

- God sent his beloved Son, Jesus, to bring all people back into his friendship.
- Jesus is the Savior and the Good Shepherd.

To learn more, go to the *Catechism of the Catholic Church* #457–458 at **usccb.org**.

People of Faith

This week, your child met Saint Cristóbal Magallanes Jara, a Mexican priest who was martyred on false charges of encouraging a revolt.

CHILDREN AT THIS AGE >>>

How They Understand God's Plan Just as there is a purpose for everything God made, there is a plan for each of our lives. God gives each of us free will because actions cannot truly be good or loving if they are not done freely. As your child learns about God's plan for his or her life, he or she will also understand that there are times when we stray from God's plan. It's important for children to know that God will help them become what he made them to be and that God always provides us a way back to himself.

CONSIDER THIS >>>

When have you ever regretted something you've said or done?

At times, we all do things that are insensitive or downright hurtful. We sin and need to be redeemed. "In our churches, we behold Jesus nailed to the Cross, an image that reminds us of his painful sacrifice to bring about the forgiveness of all our sins and guilt. ... Each time we see the crucifix, we can reflect on the infinite mercy of God, who saves us through the reconciling act of Jesus" (*USCCA, p. 243*).

LET'S TALK >>>

- Ask your child what he or she thinks it means to be responsible for your choices.
- Talk about how to react when someone thinks you have done something you didn't.

LET'S PRAY >>>

Saint Cristóbal, ask Jesus to watch over our family as a shepherd watches over his sheep. Amen.

For a multimedia glossary of Catholic Faith Words, Sunday readings, seasonal and Saint resources, and chapter activities go to **aliveinchrist.osv.com**.

Chapter 2 Review

A **Work with Words** Write the letter of the correct word or words from the Word Bank to complete each sentence.

Word Bank

a. Savior

b. Original Sin

c. Shepherd

d. Jesus

e. friendship

1. The choice of Adam and Eve to disobey God is called ☐.

2. God promised to send a ☐.

3. The Savior God sent was ☐.

4. Jesus is the Good ☐.

5. Jesus brings people back into ☐ with God.

B **Check Understanding** Fill in the circle beside the correct answer.

6. You were created in _____ image.
   ○ your friend's   ○ your own   ○ God's

7. God gave you the _____ to make choices.
   ○ responsibility   ○ freedom   ○ plan

8. All choices have results, or _____.
   ○ consequences   ○ freedom   ○ responsibility

9. _____ are responsible for the choices you make.
   ○ The Saints   ○ Others   ○ You

10. Jesus is like a shepherd and his _____ are like sheep.
    ○ friends   ○ followers   ○ parents

 Go to **aliveinchrist.osv.com** for an interactive review.

72 Chapter 2 Review

The Word of God

♡ Let Us Pray

Leader: Your Word, O God, teaches us each day.

"Your word, LORD, stands forever,
it is firm as the heavens." Psalm 119:89

All: Thank you, God, for your Word. Amen.

📖 God's Word

"And he came down with them and stood on a stretch of level ground. A great crowd of his disciples and a large number of the people … came to hear him and to be healed of their diseases." Luke 6:17–18

❓ What Do You Wonder?

- What does Jesus say to you?
- How will you listen for Jesus?

Learning about God
Where is God's Word written?

God wants people to believe in him and to love him. He wants you to remember his special love. Here is a story about God's love for his People.

God's Word

The Great Flood

Once God told Noah to build a large boat called an ark. He told Noah and his family to put all different kinds of animals on the ark, too. A great flood came, and the rains poured down for forty days. Noah's family and the animals were safe on the ark.

Then the rains stopped and the sun came out. Noah praised God for saving his family. God promised that he would always take care of his People. The rainbow was a sign of God's promise. Based on Genesis 6–9

Color in the sign of God's promise to Noah.

The Bible

You can find stories of God's love in a special book called the **Bible**. The Bible is the Word of God written in human words. God guided the human writers to write about him and his saving actions. In the Bible, God tells you about himself and his plan for you. Another name for the Bible is Sacred Scripture.

The Bible has two main parts. The **Old Testament** is the first part of the Bible. It is about the friendship between God and his People before the birth of Jesus. In this part of the Bible, there are history books, law books, poetry, stories, and songs. The story of Noah's Ark is in the Old Testament.

Catholic Faith Words

Bible the Word of God written in human words. The Bible is the holy book of the Church.

Old Testament the first part of the Bible about God and his People before Jesus was born

Share Your Faith

Think What is one thing you know about God? Write it here.

_____

_____

Share Talk with a partner about how you learned this.

75

The modern-day region of Galilee, Israel, where Jesus lived and taught.

Jesus' Message

When do you read or hear Bible stories?

Jesus knew the stories of God and his People. Jesus told many stories also. These stories helped people know and love God the Father. Jesus helped people love God by his actions, too.

1. Underline things that Jesus said and did.

2. Circle the reasons that people followed Jesus.

 **God's Word**

Jesus Teaches and Heals

Jesus went all around Galilee. He taught in the synagogues where the Jewish people studied Scripture and prayed. He told people about the Good News of God's Kingdom. He healed many people who were ill.

Jesus became well-known. People from different cities came to hear Jesus teach. They brought their friends who could not walk, and Jesus cured them. Large crowds followed Jesus wherever he went.

Based on Matthew 4:23–25

Read About Jesus

You can learn about Jesus by reading the **New Testament**. The New Testament is the second part of the Bible. It is about the life and teachings of Jesus and his followers. The first four books are called Gospels. There are also letters written by Jesus' followers to the new Christians.

Listen to God's Word

Every Sunday during Mass, you hear readings from the Old and New Testaments. You also hear God's Word when you read Bible stories with your family. You can read or act out some of these stories with family or friends. When you gather with others to learn about your faith and pray, you often hear Bible stories or psalms.

Catholic Faith Words

New Testament the second part of the Bible about the life and teachings of Jesus, his followers, and the early Church

Connect Your Faith

Write About Jesus Imagine you are talking to a group of younger children. What would you say to them about Jesus? Write three words that tell about him.

1. _____

2. _____

3. _____

Our Catholic Life

How can you learn about and share God's love?

Jesus treated people kindly. He did not care if people were young, old, healthy, or sick. He cared for all people. Jesus teaches us how to live. You can learn about God the Father's love from Jesus. Then, you can share his love.

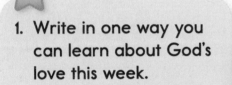

1. Write in one way you can learn about God's love this week.

2. Write in one way you will share God's love this week.

Ways to Learn about God's Love	Ways to Share God's Love
Read the Bible with our families.	Listen to our parents.
Gather with our parish to worship.	Treat people kindly.
Take part in religion class.	Tell others stories about Jesus.
Sing songs about Jesus.	Include everyone in our games.

1. _____.

2. _____.

People of Faith

Saint Luke, first century

Saint Luke was a follower of Jesus. He learned about Jesus from Saint Paul and probably the Apostles and Mary. He wrote down their stories about Jesus in what became one of the Gospels. In his Gospel, Luke talks about Jesus' birth and also how Jesus cared for people who were poor, sick, and lonely. Luke traveled with Saint Paul. He wrote down stories about their trips in another book of the Bible called the Acts of the Apostles. Luke was also a doctor and a painter.

October 18

Discuss: What is your favorite story about Jesus?

Learn more about Saint Luke at **aliveinchrist.osv.com**

Live Your Faith

Draw a Bible Story Think about a time when you heard a Bible story about God's love. Draw part of that Bible story here.

♥ **Let Us Pray**

Pray with God's Word

Gather and begin with the Sign of the Cross.

Leader: The Bible is God's holy Word.
It is as sure as the sky above.
It is as solid as the Earth below.
Let us listen, follow, and honor God's holy Word.

All: We will listen to God's Word in the Bible.

Reader: Read John 1:1–2

All: We will live by God's good Word in the Bible.

Follow the leader in a procession.
Then honor the Bible by bowing before it.

All: We will honor God's good Word in the Bible.

 Sing "Your Words Are Spirit and Life"

Your words are spirit and life, O Lord:
richer than gold, stronger than death.
Your words are spirit and life, O Lord:
life everlasting.
Based on Psalm 19:8–11: Text and Music.
© 1993 Bernadette Farrell, Published by OCP.
All rights reserved.

FAMILY+FAITH
LIVING AND LEARNING TOGETHER

YOUR CHILD LEARNED >>>

This chapter explains how the Old Testament and New Testament are the Bible, God's inspired Word.

God's Word

 Read **Luke 6:17–18** to learn more about listening to God's Word.

Catholics Believe

• God tells his People about himself through the Bible.

• The Bible is God's Word written by humans.

To learn more, go to the *Catechism of the Catholic Church* #61, 69 at **usccb.org**.

People of Faith

This week, your child met Saint Luke, author of the Gospel of Luke and the Acts of the Apostles, which recounts the story of the early Church.

CHILDREN AT THIS AGE >>>

How They Understand the Bible As Catholics we believe that the Bible is God's Word. At first, your child might have trouble understanding how Scripture is the Word of God, but was written down by human beings. Children this age might think that God somehow delivered the Bible as a book to humankind or literally dictated each word that was written.

Over time your child will understand better that the Holy Spirit inspired people of faith to write down what is in the Bible, and that Scripture reflects the culture and personalities of the writers while still transmitting God's message at its core.

CONSIDER THIS >>>

What gives you inspiration?

Did you know that "Sacred Scripture is inspired by God and is the Word of God. Therefore, God is the author of Sacred Scripture, which means he inspires the human authors, acting in and through them.... *Inspiration* is the word used for the divine assistance given to the human authors of the books of Sacred Scripture. This means that guided by the Holy Spirit, the human authors made full use of their talents and abilities while, at the same time, writing what God intended. Sacred Scripture is inspired by God and is the Word of God. Therefore, God is the author of Sacred Scripture, which means he inspired the human authors, acting in and through them" (*USCCA, p. 26–27*).

LET'S TALK >>>

• Ask your child to name one thing he or she learned about the Bible.

• Share one of your favorite stories about Jesus and any family memories you have that include the Bible.

LET'S PRAY >>>

Saint Luke, help us to always listen to each other. Amen.

For a multimedia glossary of Catholic Faith Words, Sunday readings, seasonal and Saint resources, and chapter activities go to **aliveinchrist.osv.com**.

Chapter 3 Review

A **Work with Words** Write the letter of the word or words from the Word Bank to complete each sentence.

1. The Bible is ☐ Word.

2. The New Testament tells about ☐.

3. The first part of the Bible is the ☐.

4. One name for the Bible is Sacred ☐.

5. The first four books of the ☐ Testament are the Gospels.

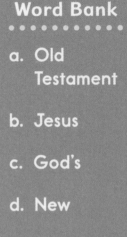

Word Bank

a. Old Testament

b. Jesus

c. God's

d. New

e. Scripture

B **Check Understanding** Circle the correct answer.

6. The Old Testament tells about _____ and his Chosen People.

   Jesus   God   Adam

7. You can read the _____ to learn about God's love.

   newspaper   hymnal   Bible

8. When you _____ you share God's love.

   are kind   are unkind   steal

9. The New Testament is about Jesus' life and _____.

   teachings   friends   pets

10. You hear God's _____ when you read Bible stories.

   songs   laugh   Word

 Go to **aliveinchrist.osv.com** for an interactive review.

A **Work with Words** Complete each sentence with the correct word from the Word Bank.

Word Bank

Bible

Jesus

Savior

God

Creation

1. The Old and New Testaments make up the _____.

2. You are made in the image and likeness of _____.

3. God's greatest gift is _____.

4. God promised to send a _____.

5. _____ is everything made by God.

B **Check Understanding** Fill in the circle beside the correct answer.

6. Who told the story of the Good Shepherd?

○ Eve   ○ John   ○ Jesus

7. What is the Word of God written in human words?

○ a book   ○ the Bible   ○ the Savior

8. Who wrote the psalms?

○ David   ○ Mary   ○ Jesus

9. Which part of the Bible is about Jesus?

○ New Testament   ○ Psalms   ○ Old Testament

10. Who guided the Bible writers?

○ humans   ○ Adam   ○ God

Unit Review

Draw a line from Column A to the best ending in Column B.

Column A	Column B
11. Humans are	the holy book of the Church.
12. The Bible is	your choices.
13. You are responsible for	the most special part of God's creation.
14. You can learn about God by	all people.
15. Jesus cared for	reading the Bible.

C **Make Connections** Circle the correct answer.

16. _____ is the sin committed by Adam and Eve.

Old Sin   Original lie   Original Sin

17. _____ is the name of Jesus that tells you God is his Father.

Son of God   Christ   Good Shepherd

18. Choosing to disobey God on purpose is a _____.

sin   friend   teaching

19. The first four books of the New Testament are called _____.

Acts   Letters   Gospels

20. The _____ Testament tells about God and his People before Jesus was born.

New   Old   Original

Write the name or names that best answer the question.

21. I was a king of God's people. I wrote poems of praise and thanks to God. Who am I?

_____

22. We lived in the Garden called Eden. We disobeyed God. Who are we?

_____

23. I am the Good Shepherd. I lead God's People back to him. Who am I?

_____

24. I built an ark that saved my family from a flood. Who am I?

_____

25. I guided the Bible writers. Who am I?

_____

Trinity

Our Catholic Tradition

- There are three Divine Persons in the Holy Trinity. (CCC, 253)

- God the Father loves and cares for us. (CCC, 239)

- We can trust and rely on God the Father. (CCC, 322)

- Jesus, the Son of God, sets an example for us with his life and teachings. (CCC, 561)

- God the Holy Spirit guides the Church and helps us to be holy. (CCC, 747)

How does the Sign of the Cross remind us of the Holy Trinity?

God the Father

 ## Let Us Pray

Leader: God, you call us to be your children.

God said to me: "You are my child;
today I have created you." **Based on Psalm 2:7**

All: God, please bless us today and every day. Amen.

 ## God's Word

"…do not seek what you are to eat and what you are to drink, and do not worry anymore. All the nations of the world seek for these things, and your Father knows that you need them. Instead, seek his kingdom, and these other things will be given you besides." **Luke 12:29–31**

? What Do You Wonder?

- How do you know God?
- Why do we call God our Father?

Care for God's Children

How does God care for you?

This is a story about a priest who made a home for children in need.

Saint John Bosco

Lorenzo and Giovanni huddled alone in the shadows. They heard mothers and fathers calling for their children. Nobody called their names. Father John Bosco found the boys cold and in the dark. They told Father John that many other children lived alone on the streets.

"I will start a home for the children of the streets. I will teach them how to read, fix things, and pray," said Father John.

Father John helped many homeless children to feel loved. He taught them that God is everyone's Father. He led a holy life and after he died, he was named a **Saint**.

➤ **What do you think Father John's home for children was like?**

Catholic Faith Words

Saint a hero of the Church who loved God very much, led a holy life, and is now with God in Heaven

God the Father the First Divine Person of the Holy Trinity

© Our Sunday Visitor

God the Father

Father John Bosco treated the young children like they were his own. He showed them love and taught them about God, like Jesus did.

Jesus taught about his Father's great love. You call God "Father" because he created you and cares for you. He cares for everyone. **God the Father** loves you as a good parent does.

"I will never forget you.
See, upon the palms of my hands
I have engraved you." Isaiah 49:15–16

Share Your Faith

Think Trace the outline of your hand. Write one way that you know God cares for you.

Share With a partner, talk about ways you can thank God.

The Father's Love

What does it mean to trust in God?

Jesus told people not to worry too much. He said that God the Father wants you to have everything you need.

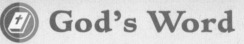

🕮 God's Word

Rely on God

Do not worry about what you will eat or wear. Life is more important than food and clothing. Look at the birds in the sky. They do not plant their food; they do not gather grain, yet your heavenly Father feeds them. Are you not more important than they? Learn from the way the wild flowers grow. They do not work or spin, but they are beautiful. If God cares so much for the grass of the field, how much more will he take care of you? Do not worry. Your heavenly Father knows what you need. Based on Matthew 6:25–32

© Our Sunday Visitor

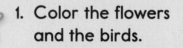

1. Color the flowers and the birds.

2. Draw yourself into the picture.

Turn to God in Prayer

Jesus told his followers to pray to the Father for whatever they might need. In your **prayer**, you will be talking to and listening to God the Father as Jesus did. Sometimes we say God or Lord when we pray to God the Father.

Jesus knew that you can always **trust** God. You can always depend on God and know that he wants what is best for you. God, your loving Father, is always listening.

Catholic Faith Words

prayer talking to and listening to God

trust to believe in and depend on someone

Connect Your Faith

Pray to God Unscramble the words below to find the first lines of the prayer Jesus taught us.

ROU HERFAT,
OHW TRA NI
VANHEE,
WODLELAH EB
HTY MENA

our father,
who art in
heaven,
hallowed be
thy name.

God the Father **91**

Our Catholic Life

What does it mean to have trust?

When you love or respect someone, you trust in him or her. You believe that the person will do what is best for you. You know you can depend on that person in good times and bad times.

Sometimes, people you trust may let you down, even though they do not mean to. That is because we are human. But you can always depend on God. You are his child. He is with you every day. You can trust God to love you and care for you.

Match the people on the left with one thing you can trust them to do.

People in Your Life	You Can Trust Them
Family Members	to protect you
Friends	to love you and take care of you
Teachers	to help you grow closer to God
Crossing Guards and Police Officers	to help you learn
Members of Your Parish Family	to play fair and treat you kindly

People of Faith

Julian of Norwich, 1342–c.1430

Julian lived in a town in England called Norwich. She loved to pray. She prayed by talking to God like she talked to her mother or father. Julian said that the whole world was like a little nut in God's hand. When we pray, we don't have to worry because God will always take care of us. Even when we are unhappy, God watches over us. Julian said that we should ask God for help in all we do. She was the first woman to write a book in English. It was about God's love.

May 13

Discuss: How does God care for you?

Learn more about Julian of Norwich at **aliveinchrist.osv.com**

Live Your Faith

Find the Message Circle the red letters. Then copy the circled letters in order on the lines below for a special message.

E G D F M O	K R N J L O	A C T Y Z W	X T O M N R	V K R C B Y
C V G L L O	Z A D R T W	V M I S S L	N L L R S T	C B A M M K
U S E A B C	C B A Q V R	L M E D E O	P Z F M M Y	M N O H K U

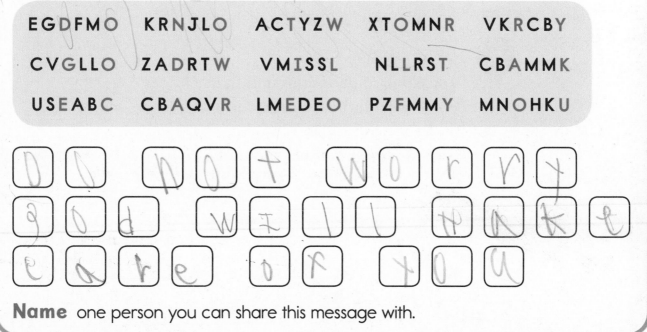

D D D O T W O r r Y
g O d W I l l H A K e
e a r e O r Y O U

Name one person you can share this message with.

♥ **Let Us Pray**

Asking Prayer

Gather and begin with the
Sign of the Cross.

Leader: Let us pray for those
who need God's help.

All: Lord, hear our prayer.

Leader: For people who have lost
their homes, let us pray to
the Lord.

All: Lord, hear our prayer.

Leader: For people who are far from their families,
let us pray to the Lord.

All: Lord, hear our prayer.

Leader: For help to care for others as Jesus did,
let us pray to the Lord.

All: Lord, hear our prayers.

 Sing "People Worry"

People worry about this and that.
People worry about this and that!
But Jesus tells us, "Don't worry.
Don't worry about this and that!"

©1994, Christopher Walker and Paule Freeburg, DC. Published by OCP. All rights reserved.

© Our Sunday Visitor

FAMILY+FAITH
LIVING AND LEARNING TOGETHER

YOUR CHILD LEARNED >>>

This chapter explores God the Father's love and the importance of prayer to deepen our relationship with him.

God's Word

Read **Luke 12:29–31** and see why God doesn't want us to worry.

Catholics Believe

- God is our Father who created us and cares for us.
- We can trust in God because he loves us.

To learn more, go to the *Catechism of the Catholic Church* #322, 2780–2782 at **usccb.org**.

People of Faith

This week, your child met Blessed Julian of Norwich who said that all "shall be well" for those who trust in God.

CHILDREN AT THIS AGE >>>

How They Understand God the Father God reveals himself as a loving father. Second-graders who have good fathers at home will be able to relate to this and connect it with an understanding of God's love for us. Alternatively, if a child has no father in the home, or if they have had negative experiences with a father figure, they might have difficulty integrating the concept of God as a father. Knowing how God intends for parents to care for their children can help with this understanding, and knowing God as a perfect Father can become a particular source of comfort and hope to these children.

CONSIDER THIS >>>

How important is trust in a relationship?

Without trust there is not even the possibility of relationship. Throughout the Old Testament there is a growing understanding of the special relationship between God and the Israelites as they learn to trust ever more deeply in the providential care of God. "Jesus' revelation of God as his Father flows from a profound awareness not only of that same providential care but also of an indescribable intimacy." (cf., e.g., Jn14) (*USCCA, p. 484–485*).

LET'S TALK >>>

- Ask your child to name people your family trusts. Discuss why.
- Share a time when you knew God was really there for you. Talk about how depending on and trusting in God made a difference for you or the family.

LET'S PRAY >>>

"All shall be well and all shall be well and all manner of thing shall be well." (Prayer of Blessed Julian of Norwich)

For a multimedia glossary of Catholic Faith Words, Sunday readings, seasonal and Saint resources, and chapter activities go to **aliveinchrist.osv.com**.

Chapter 4 Review

A **Work With Words** Fill in the blank with the correct word from the Word Bank.

Word Bank

trust

cares

Father

depend

prayer

1. God _____ for everyone.

2. Jesus taught you to call God the

   _____.

3. _____ God.

4. _____ is talking to and

   listening to God.

5. You can always _____ on God.

B **Check Understanding** Complete each sentence in Column A with the letter of the correct word or words in Column B.

Column A

6. A ⬜ is a holy person who obeyed God.

7. Jesus told people not to ⬜.

8. Jesus taught about ⬜.

9. We love and ⬜ the people we trust.

10. God loves you and wants what is ⬜.

Column B

a. respect

b. his Father's great love

c. Saint

d. best for you

e. worry too much

Go to **aliveinchrist.osv.com** for an interactive review.

96 Chapter 4 Review

God the Son

 Let Us Pray

Leader: God the Father, show us your Son.

As a father has compassion on his children,
so the LORD has compassion on those
who honor him.   **Based on Psalm 103:13**

All: Thank you, God, for sending your Son
to show us the way to you. Amen.

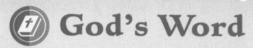 **God's Word**

"After all the people had been baptized and Jesus
also had been baptized and was praying, heaven
was opened and the holy Spirit descended upon him
in bodily form like a dove. And a voice came from
heaven, 'You are my beloved Son; with you I am
well pleased.'"   Luke 3:21–22

? What Do You Wonder?

• What does Jesus want you to do?

• How do you live like Jesus?

A Savior Is Born

What did the angel tell Mary?

© Our Sunday Visitor

Catholic Faith Words

Mary the Mother of Jesus, the Mother of God. She is also called "Our Lady" because she is our Mother and the Mother of the Church.

angel a type of spiritual being that does God's work, such as delivering messages from God or helping to keep people safe from harm

All names have special meanings. Long ago, God sent his only Son to Earth. God sent him to show all people how they should live. God chose **Mary** to be his Son's Mother. His Son had a special name.

God sent the Angel Gabriel to Mary in the town of Nazareth. The **angel** told Mary that she would give birth to a son and that she would name him Jesus, which means, "God saves."

1. Draw a square around the Angel Gabriel on the left.

2. Draw a circle around Mary and Jesus on the right.

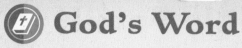

God's Word

Announcing Jesus' Birth

When the Angel Gabriel visited Mary he said, "He will be great and will be called Son of the Most High." Mary didn't understand how this could happen to her.

The angel said in reply, "The holy Spirit and the power of the Most High will come over you. Therefore the child to be born will be called holy, the Son of God." Mary told the angel, "May it be done to me as you say."

Months later, Jesus was born in Bethlehem. There were shepherds nearby caring for their flock. An angel of the Lord appeared to them in a great light. The shepherds were frightened.

The angel said, "Do not be afraid. Behold, I have Good News of great joy for all people. Today a savior has been born!" Based on Luke 1:26–38; 2:1–11

Share Your Faith

Think Write or draw your favorite part of the story inside the star.

Share with a partner.

The Holy Family
How did Jesus set an example for others?

Mary and Joseph brought Jesus back to Nazareth where he grew up. Together, they are called the **Holy Family**. Like most children, Jesus loved to learn and play. But Jesus was also very different, he was the Son of God.

Catholic Faith Words

Holy Family the name for the human family of Jesus, Mary, and Joseph

God's Word

The Boy Jesus in the Temple

When Jesus was twelve, Mary and Joseph took him to Jerusalem for a holy day. On their way home, Joseph and Mary noticed that Jesus was missing. They were very worried and went back to Jerusalem to find him.

They found Jesus sitting with wise teachers in the Temple. Jesus' questions and answers amazed everyone in the temple.

Jesus came back to Nazareth and obeyed his parents. He grew in age, in learning, and in holiness. Based on Luke 2:41–52

➤ What is one thing Jesus might have told the wise teachers about God?

Jesus Begins His Work

When Jesus was thirty years old, he went to see his cousin John, whom we call John the Baptist. John wanted all sinners to turn toward God. He baptized them with water in the Jordan River.

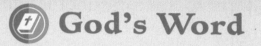 God's Word

Baptism of Jesus

One day, Jesus asked John to baptize him. Jesus never sinned. But he wanted to set an example for others. After Jesus' baptism, the Holy Spirit came down on him in the form of a dove. Then a voice from Heaven said, "You are my beloved Son. I am pleased with you."

After this, Jesus taught about God his Father and shared his Father's love with everyone.

Based on Matthew 3:13–17

We learn about God the Father from the people in our families.

➤ **Who teaches you about God the Father?**

Connect Your Faith

Circle the Words Circle the names for Jesus and mark an X on the words that aren't. What's your favorite name for Jesus?

Good Shepherd   Savior

John   God the Son

God the Cousin

_____

Our Catholic Life

What does Jesus teach us about loving God and others?

After his baptism, Jesus traveled throughout his country to remind others that God loved them. He taught them to love one another and to be good to others.

Jesus still teaches us today through the Bible, the Church, the Sacraments, and his followers. Listen carefully and you will learn how to show your love for God and others.

Fill in the blanks with things you can say to follow Jesus' teachings.

What Jesus Teaches	Things You Can Say
Forgive other people.	I forgive you.
Be kind to others.	_____
Help people who are sick.	May I come visit you?
Share with others.	I'll share this orange with you.
Pray often.	_____

102 Chapter 5

People of Faith

Saint Peter, first century

Saint Peter was a fisherman with his brother Saint Andrew. Later, he was the leader of Jesus' followers. He knew that Jesus was the Son of God. But he also knew Jesus was a man. He ate with Jesus. He prayed with Jesus. He walked and talked with Jesus. He even went to parties with Jesus! Saint Peter knew that Jesus got tired and hungry. He knew when Jesus was happy and sad. But most of all, he knew that Jesus loved everyone. After Jesus died, Saint Peter told many people about Jesus. He is considered to be the first Pope.

June 29

Discuss: What do you think Jesus might have done for fun?

 Learn more about Saint Peter at **aliveinchrist.osv.com**

Live Your Faith

Meet Jesus Choose one of the events shown and act out what Jesus might be saying. What would you say to Jesus if you were there?

baptism

Teaching

Praying

God the Son **103**

♡ Let Us Pray

Signing Prayer

Gather and begin with the Sign of the Cross.

Leader: Father, you sent us your only Son,
giving him "the name that is above
every name" (Philippians 2:9), the
name that means "God saves."
Accept our prayer of praise and thanks for

All: Sign and pray—Jesus,

Leader: the Redeemer who became one of us;

All: Sign and pray—Jesus,

Leader: who taught us in word and example;

All: Sign and pray—Jesus,

Leader: who suffered and celebrated with us;

All: Sign and pray—Jesus,

Leader: who died for us and rose to save us;

All: Sign and pray—Jesus,

Leader: in whose name we give glory to you,
O God, now and forever.

▶ **All:** Sing "You are God"

Jesus, you are God.
There is none like you.
Jesus, you are God,
and we worship you.

© 2011, Banner Kidd.
Published by Our Sunday Visitor, Inc.

FAMILY+FAITH
LIVING AND LEARNING TOGETHER

YOUR CHILD LEARNED >>>

This chapter explores the Holy Family and Jesus' life on Earth.

God's Word

 Go to **Luke 3:21–22** to read what happened at the baptism of Jesus.

Catholics Believe

- Jesus is the beloved Son of God born of Mary.
- Jesus is the Savior of the world who showed us God the Father's love.

To learn more, go to the *Catechism of the Catholic Church* #452–454 at **usccb.org**.

People of Faith

This week, your child met Saint Peter, who knew Jesus both as God and man.

CHILDREN AT THIS AGE >>>

How They Understand Jesus, God's Son Second-graders have often already heard many stories of Jesus. Because the Gospel stories offer few glimpses into Jesus' childhood (only infancy and age 12), it might be hard for your child to picture Jesus as a child his or her age. It is important for children this age to know that Jesus was also seven and eight years old, and that they can follow him in the choices they make right now. Their understanding of this will grow as you point out daily opportunities to be like Jesus through the choices your child makes.

CONSIDER THIS >>>

How is love made visible in your family?

The love visible in your family begins in the heart of God. "... Christ's command to love is the door to the whole supernatural order. At the same time, it encourages [us] to know that Jesus affirms the human good of each person. Together [we] must seek the same goals of mutual love united to Christ's love, the raising of a family and the continued growth of [our] relationship" (*USCCA, p. 286*).

LET'S TALK >>>

- Ask your child what stories about Jesus he or she heard this week (Jesus' birth, childhood, and baptism).
- Share what teaching of Jesus you remember learning about as a child and how it is still important to you today.

LET'S PRAY >>>

Saint Peter, pray for us that we may come to know and love Jesus as much as you did. Amen.

For a multimedia glossary of Catholic Faith Words, Sunday readings, seasonal and Saint resources, and chapter activities go to **aliveinchrist.osv.com**.

Chapter 5 Review

 A **Work with Words** Write the letter of the correct word or words from the Word Bank to complete the sentence.

Word Bank

a. the Holy Family

b. John

c. Son of God

d. Jesus

e. The Angel Gabriel

1. Jesus is the ☐.

2. ☐ told Mary about being the Mother of God's Son.

3. ☐ is the Savior of the world.

4. ☐ was Jesus' cousin.

5. Mary, Joseph, and Jesus are ☐.

B **Check Understanding** Make a list of five things Jesus teaches us. Write the word that is missing from each teaching.

6. _____ other people.

7. Be _____ to others.

8. _____ people who are sick.

9. _____ with others.

10. _____ often.

Go to **aliveinchrist.osv.com** for an interactive review.

God the Holy Spirit

♥ Let Us Pray

Leader: God, send us your Holy Spirit.

"May your kind spirit guide me." Psalm 143:10

All: Holy Spirit, be with us always. Amen.

📖 God's Word

"And [behold] I am sending the promise of my Father upon you; but stay in the city until you are clothed with power from on high."

Luke 24:49

❓ What Do You Wonder?

- What does the Holy Spirit look like?
- How do you know the Holy Spirit is with you?

Color in the stained glass frame around the image of the Holy Spirit.

One in Three
Who is the Holy Trinity?

You cannot see the wind, but you know that it is there. You cannot see God the **Holy Spirit** either, but you can see what the Spirit does.

Catholic Faith Words

Holy Spirit the Third Divine Person of the Holy Trinity

Holy Trinity the one God in three Divine Persons—God the Father, God the Son, and God the Holy Spirit

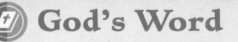 **God's Word**

The Promise

Jesus knew he would be returning to his Father in Heaven. He wanted his followers to continue his work.

Jesus promised his followers, "The Advocate, the holy Spirit that the Father will send in my name—he will teach you everything and remind you of all that [I] told you." Based on John 14:15–26

108 Chapter 6

Father, Son, and Holy Spirit

Jesus teaches you that God is the Father of all. Jesus is the Son of God. And the Holy Spirit, sent from the Father and the Son, is also God.

But there are not three gods. There is only one God, who is Father, Son, and Holy Spirit. The Church's name for the one God in three Divine Persons is the **Holy Trinity**.

God the Father is the First Person of the Holy Trinity. God the Son became man in Jesus Christ. He is the Second Person of the Holy Trinity. God the Holy Spirit is the Third Person of the Holy Trinity.

Believing in the Holy Trinity is the most important part of your faith and you show your belief when you make the Sign of the Cross.

Share Your Faith

Think Choose a color for each Person of the Holy Trinity, then color or decorate the circles using the colors you have chosen.

Share Talk about your picture with a partner.

God the Father

God the Son

God the Holy Spirit

God the Holy Spirit **109**

Guided by the Spirit

How is the Holy Spirit with us today?

Jesus' followers are called his **disciples**. Before he returned to Heaven, he told them his plan.

God's Word

The Spirit Comes

Jesus told his disciples to wait for the promise of the Father that he had told them about. He said, "You will receive power when the holy Spirit comes upon you, and you will be my witnesses in Jerusalem . . . and to the ends of the earth."

The Twelve disciples and some other followers of Jesus stayed in Jerusalem and prayed. Soon the Holy Spirit came. Suddenly a noise like a strong driving wind came from the sky, and it filled the entire house in which they were gathered. Then tongues of fire appeared to them, which parted and came to rest on each one of them. This day is called Pentecost.

Based on Acts 1:4–5, 8; 2:2–3

Underline the ways the Holy Spirit came to the disciples on the day of Pentecost.

© Our Sunday Visitor

The Holy Spirit Today

After the Holy Spirit came to them at **Pentecost**, Jesus' Twelve closest disciples were guided to continue his work. They became known as his **Apostles**.

The Holy Spirit comes today through the Church's Sacraments, prayer, and in God's Word. The Holy Spirit guides the Church and makes Jesus' disciples holy. He helps you make good decisions and grow more loving.

Disciples of Jesus

Jesus' disciples are in every part of the world. The Holy Spirit teaches us all how to pray. The Spirit helps today's disciples remember and understand the stories of Jesus. You are learning to be a disciple of Jesus.

© Our Sunday Visitor

Catholic Faith Words

disciples followers of Jesus who believe in him and live by his teachings

Pentecost fifty days after the Resurrection when the Holy Spirit first came upon the Twelve disciples and the Church

Apostles the Twelve disciples Jesus chose to be his closest followers. After the coming of the Holy Spirit, they shared in his work and mission in a special way.

Connect Your Faith

Circle the Places Circle each place on the map where the Holy Spirit helps you be a disciple of Jesus.

God the Holy Spirit **111**

Our Catholic Life

What does it mean to follow Jesus?

Jesus' first followers were his friends. They traveled with Jesus and listened to his stories. They saw how Jesus treated others. Jesus asked his Apostles and other disciples to help others learn about God's love.

You are Jesus' friend and follower, too. He wants you to listen to him and to live the way he lived. Being a disciple of Jesus means following his example.

Ways to Follow Jesus

- Pray to God the Father.
- Ask God the Holy Spirit to guide you.
- Think of other people, not only of yourself.
- Be fair to your family members and friends.
- Help people who are in need.

In the footprint, write or draw one way you can follow Jesus' example today.

Be kind and you to other (an help others and go to mass (worship god)

People of Faith

Saint Arnold Janssen, 1837–1909

January 15

Saint Arnold Janssen was a German priest. He wanted everybody to know about Jesus. He helped priests and sisters, serving as missionaries, build churches all around the world. They went to faraway places like China. Saint Arnold prayed to the Holy Spirit to help with his work. He asked some religious sisters to help him pray. These sisters took turns praying all day and night for the missionaries. Today, sisters like these are sometimes called "Pink Sisters" because they wear pink habits.

Discuss: What do you pray to the Holy Spirit for?

 Learn more about Saint Arnold at **aliveinchrist.osv.com**

Live Your Faith

Learn by Heart
Memorize the Prayer for the Holy Spirit.

Come, Holy Spirit, fill the hearts of your faithful. And kindle in them the fire of your love.

Send forth your Spirit and they will be created. And you will renew the face of the earth.

113

Let Us Pray

Prayer for the Holy Spirit

Gather and begin with the Sign of the Cross.

Leader: Let us sing as we ask God to send the Holy Spirit to us each day.
In our family...

All: Send us your Spirit, O Lord.

Leader: With our classmates...

All: Send us your Spirit, O Lord.

Leader: In all that we say and do...

All: Send us your Spirit, O Lord.

Leader: We ask this in Jesus' name.

All: Amen.

 Sing "The Holy Spirit"

The Holy Spirit, sent from God above.
The Holy Spirit, bringing peace and love.
Receive the power of the Holy Spirit today!

The Holy Spirit, giving strength each day.
The Holy Spirit, showing us the way.
Receive the power of the Holy Spirit today!
© 2008, John Burland. All rights reserved.

FAMILY+FAITH
LIVING AND LEARNING TOGETHER

YOUR CHILD LEARNED >>>

This chapter explains that Jesus promised to send the Holy Spirit to be our helper and guide.

God's Word

 Read **Acts 2:1–4** to find out about the coming of the Holy Spirit on the first Pentecost.

Catholics Believe

- The Holy Spirit guides the Church and helps you to be a disciple.
- The Holy Trinity is one God in three Divine Persons.

To learn more, go to the *Catechism of the Catholic Church* #237, 243 at **usccb.org**.

People of Faith

This week, your child met Saint Arnold Janssen, a German priest with a special devotion to the Holy Spirit.

CHILDREN AT THIS AGE >>>

How They Understand God the Holy Spirit The Holy Spirit might still be difficult for your child to understand, but children this age are growing in their understanding that the Holy Spirit lives in their heart. Because cause and effect is so important to children this age, reflecting on the Gifts and Fruits of the Spirit can help second-graders see the work of the Holy Spirit in their own lives. Talk with your child about the Fruits and Gifts of the Spirit (See the We Live section in the back of your book.), and point out times when you see examples in their actions.

CONSIDER THIS >>>

Imagine being invited somewhere you really want to go.

The greatest invitation we ever get is the invitation to spend all of eternity with God. "'Heaven is the ultimate end and fulfillment of the deepest human longings, the state of supreme, definitive happiness' (CCC, no. 1024). This will be brought about by a perfect communion with the Holy Trinity, the Blessed Mother, the angels and saints. Jesus Christ opened heaven to us by his death and Resurrection" (*USCCA, p. 153*).

LET'S TALK >>>

- Have your child describe who the Holy Spirit is and what he does.
- Name some ways your family can be followers of Jesus.

LET'S PRAY >>>

Guard me, ... O Holy Spirit, that I always may be holy. (Prayer of Saint Augustine)

For a multimedia glossary of Catholic Faith Words, Sunday readings, seasonal and Saint resources, and chapter activities go to **aliveinchrist.osv.com**.

Chapter 6 Review

A **Work With Words** Complete each sentence with the correct word or words from the Word Bank.

1. The Holy Spirit came to the disciples as [wind]

2. The [trinty] is one God in three Divine Persons.

3. The Holy Spirit helps us make good [decisions]

4. The day the Holy Spirit came is called [Pentecost sunday]

5. The Twelve disciples became known as Jesus' [Apostles] after the Holy Spirit came to them.

B **Check Understanding** Fill in the circle beside the correct answer.

6. You show belief in the Holy Trinity when you make the ____.
   - ⦿ Sign of the Cross
   - ○ sign of love
   - ○ sign of peace

7. Being a disciple of Jesus means following his ____.
   - ○ orders
   - ○ trail
   - ⦿ example

8. To follow Jesus, you need to think of ____.
   - ⦿ other people
   - ○ yourself
   - ○ only your friends

9. Jesus asked his Apostles to help others learn about ____.
   - ○ animals
   - ○ creation
   - ⦿ God's love

10. The ____ guides the Church.
    - ○ Holy Friends
    - ⦿ Holy Spirit
    - ○ Holy Week

© Our Sunday Visitor

Go to **aliveinchrist.osv.com** for an interactive review.

A **Work with Words** Complete each sentence with the letter of the correct word or words from the Word Bank.

Word Bank

a. Holy Spirit

b. disciples

c. Holy Trinity

d. Father

e. prayer

1. People who follow Jesus are called [b].

2. Jesus promised to send the [a].

3. Listening and talking to God is called [e]. *prayer*

4. Jesus taught us to call God [d]. *Father*

5. The one God in three Divine Persons is called the [c]. *Holy Trinity*

B **Check Understanding** Draw a line from the descriptions in Column A to the correct names in Column B.

Column A

Column B

6. The Third Person of the Holy Trinity

7. The Mother of God's Son

8. The First Person of the Holy Trinity

9. A Saint who helped homeless boys

10. The Second Person of the Holy Trinity

Mary

John Bosco

God the Holy Spirit

God the Son

God the Father

Fill in the circle beside the correct answer.

11. You can always ____ God to love you.

○ respect ○ trust ○ know

12. After Jesus was ____ he traveled the country where he lived.

○ baptized ○ older ○ risen

13. Jesus teaches today through the ____.

○ Church ○ town ○ Earth

14. You can follow Jesus by ____ people.

○ mistreating ○ forgetting ○ forgiving

15. A ____ of Jesus follows his example.

○ enemy ○ Saint ○ disciple

C **Make Connections** Complete each sentence below.

16. A Saint is a holy person who _____.

17. Prayer is talking to and _____.

18. To trust is to believe in and _____.

19. Disciples are people who choose

_____.

20. The Apostles are the Twelve _____.

Write the name or names that best answer the question.

21. I am the Mother of the Church. Who am I?

_____

22. When I was a boy my parents were looking for me and found me in the Temple talking to the wise teachers. Who am I?

_____

23. I baptized my cousin Jesus in the Jordan River. Who am I?

_____

24. You receive me in the Church's Sacraments and I help you pray. Who am I?

_____

25. Together we make up the Holy Family. Who are we?

_____

Jesus Christ

Our Catholic Tradition

- God gave Moses the Ten Commandments to help us know how to live in love. (CCC, 2077)

- Jesus gave us a New Commandment to love as he loves us. (CCC, 1970)

- Our conscience is a gift from God that helps us make choices about right and wrong. (CCC, 1777–1778)

- Jesus teaches us that God our Father always offers forgiveness and shows us mercy. (CCC, 545)

Why do we depend on Jesus' promise for mercy and forgiveness?

© Our Sunday Visitor

God's Commandments

♥ Let Us Pray

Leader: Dear God, help us to know and follow your truth.

"Open my eyes to see clearly
the wonders of your law....
do not hide your commandments from
me." Psalm 119:18–19

All: Thank you, God, for showing us how to
follow you. Amen.

✝ God's Word

"The LORD said to Moses: Come up to me on the mountain and, while you are there, I will give you the stone tablets on which I have written the commandments intended for their instruction."

Exodus 24:12

? What Do You Wonder?

- Who gives you the rules to live by every day?
- Why do people need rules?

The Ten Commandments

What can help me to make good choices?

God gave Moses and his Chosen People some laws to help them. These laws are called the **Ten Commandments**. God wants you to follow these laws, too. They help you make good choices about your friendship with God and others.

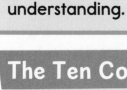

Check two things you need help understanding.

The Ten Commandments	How You Can Live Them
1 I am the LORD your God: you shall not have strange Gods before me.	☐ Make God the most important thing in your life.
2 You shall not take the name of the LORD your God in vain.	☐ Use God's name in a reverent way.
3 Remember to keep holy the LORD's Day.	☐ Attend Mass and rest on Sunday.
4 Honor your father and your mother.	☐ Love and obey your parents and guardians.
5 You shall not kill.	☐ Be kind to people and animals.
6 You shall not commit adultery.	☑ Be respectful in the things you do with your body.
7 You shall not steal.	☐ Don't take other people's things.
8 You shall not bear false witness against your neighbor.	☐ Tell the truth.
9 You shall not covet your neighbor's wife.	☑ Keep your thoughts and words clean.
10 You shall not covet your neighbor's goods.	☐ Be happy with the things you have; don't be jealous of what others have.

Jesus' Commands

Jesus learned and followed the Ten Commandments. When he grew up, Jesus taught a Commandment called the **Great Commandment**. It includes all the other Commandments and sums up God's laws.

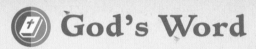

God's Word

"You shall love the Lord, your God, with all your heart, with all your being, with all your strength, and with all your mind, and your neighbor as yourself." Luke 10:27

© Our Sunday Visitor

God's Commandments teach us how to live and show love. Learning about his Commandments helps us grow closer to him. It also helps us prepare for the Sacrament of Penance and Reconciliation.

➜ **How do you show love for God?**

Catholic Faith Words

Ten Commandments
God's laws that tell people how to love him and others

Great Commandment
the law to love God above all else and to love others the way you love yourself.

Share Your Faith

Think Pick one Commandment and write some ways you can follow it.

_____

_____

_____

Share Talk about it in a small group.

The New Commandment
What does Jesus ask us to do?

Jesus told many stories, or parables, to teach his followers that loving God means loving our neighbor. Here is a **parable** he told.

Catholic Faith Words

parable a short story Jesus told about everyday life to teach something about God

New Commandment Jesus' command for his disciples to love one another as he has loved us

✝ God's Word

The Parable of the Good Samaritan

Once a man asked Jesus, "Who is my neighbor?" Jesus told this story to answer him.

A man was going along a road alone. Robbers came and beat him up. They took everything he had and ran away, leaving him half-dead.

A Jewish priest was going down the same road. When he saw the man, he ignored him.

Later, someone who took care of the Temple came along. When he saw the man, he also ignored him.

Then a man from Samaria came along and saw the man lying on the roadside. He hurried over to help. The Samaritan bandaged the man's sores and took him to an inn. The Samaritan gave the innkeeper two silver coins to help take care of the man.

Then Jesus asked, "Which of the three was a neighbor to the robber's victim?" The man said, "The one who treated him with mercy."

Jesus said, "Go and do likewise." Luke 10:29–37

This story shows that a neighbor is any person who is in need. The Samaritan saw a man who needed help. He showed him kindness and respect. Jesus tells us how we should treat each other. We are to love one another as he has loved us. This is called the **New Commandment**.

Connect Your Faith

Act It Out Plan a Good Samaritan skit.

1. Make notes for each part and include some props.

2. Take turns acting out different roles.

What good or bad choices were made in this story?

Our Catholic Life

How can you be a good neighbor?

In the story of the Good Samaritan, Jesus taught that neighbors aren't just the people who live next door to you. All people are neighbors. A neighbor can be someone who is in need, like the man who was robbed. A neighbor can be someone who helps, like the Samaritan.

As followers of Christ, how are we to treat God? As neighbors, how are we to treat one another? The Great Commandment and Jesus' New Commandment tell us.

Write one way you love God and one way you can love your neighbor.

The Great Commandment	The New Commandment
"Love God above all things, and love your neighbor as you love yourself."	"Love one another as I have loved you."
Spend time with God every day in prayer.	Don't judge people by how they look or by how many things they have.
Thank him for all he has given us.	Reach out to people who are lonely.
Grow closer to him by learning more about him.	When someone asks you for forgiveness, give it gladly.

People of Faith

Saint Elizabeth of Hungary, 1207–1231

November 17

Saint Elizabeth was a princess of Hungary. Jesus' command to love one another was very important to Elizabeth. She spent her entire life caring for people who were poor and suffering. Elizabeth fed the hungry by giving them food at the castle gate. She sold her jewels and used the money to build hospitals. When her husband died, she was very sad. She worked hard to take care of her four children, but she kept helping the poor, too.

Discuss: What have you donated to those in need?

Learn more about Saint Elizabeth at **aliveinchrist.osv.com**

Live Your Faith

Love Others Give two examples of people who are your neighbors and how you help each other.

1. _Looking for my Parents._

2. _____

127

❤ **Let Us Pray**

Prayer of Praise

Gather and begin with the Sign of the Cross.

Leader: Jesus, you tell us you are the Way, the Truth, and the Life.

See John 14:6.

All: we praise and honor you.

Leader: You show us the way to the Father,

All: we praise and honor you.

Leader: You teach us the truth about love,

All: we praise and honor you.

Leader: You give us hope and life,

All: we praise and honor you.

Leader: Help us, Lord, to love as you do, fully and completely.

All: Amen.

 Sing "Loving God"

Love the Lord, your God,
with all your heart,
with all your soul,
with all your mind,
and with all your strength.

Text and music by Nathan Heironimus.
© 2010, Our Sunday Visitor, Inc

© Our Sunday Visitor

FAMILY+FAITH
LIVING AND LEARNING TOGETHER

YOUR CHILD LEARNED >>>

This chapter explains that the Ten Commandments teach us how to love God above all things and to love others. They are summed up in the Great Commandment.

God's Word

 Read **Exodus 24:12** to learn what God said to Moses about the Ten Commandments.

Catholics Believe

- The Ten Commandments are God's laws to his People.
- Jesus teaches you to love God above all things and love others as you love yourself.

To learn more, go to the *Catechism of the Catholic Church* #830, 2053 at **usccb.org**.

People of Faith

This week, your child met Saint Elizabeth of Hungary, a princess who used her wealth to feed the hungry and build hospitals for the sick.

CHILDREN AT THIS AGE >>>

How They Understand the Great Commandment
Second-graders are just beginning to move out of the self-centered tendencies of earlier childhood. But in a society so focused on individual comfort and fulfillment, it can be counter-cultural to speak of putting God over everything else or loving others as much as one loves one's self. Your child will need much guidance to understand how this translates into the practical decisions he or she makes every day. Much of this guidance will come in the form of the example you provide of caring for others and prioritizing God over other things.

CONSIDER THIS >>>

How do the rules in your home help you to love each other?

Children might think that rules restrict our freedom, but in actuality they lead us to reap the benefits of a deeper love. "… God has given us the virtue of love, the very love that he has for us. Our Lord asks us to accept this love and respond to him with it. Jesus made the love of God the first of the two greatest Commandments: 'You shall love the Lord, your God, with all your heart, with all your soul, and with all your mind (Matthew 22:37)'" *(USCCA, p. 343).*

LET'S TALK >>>

- Talk about family rules and why they are important.
- Ask your child what rules God gives us (Ten Commandments) and what Jesus commands us to do (to love one another as he has loved us).

LET'S PRAY >>>

Saint Elizabeth, pray for us that we always love our neighbors as ourselves. Amen.

For a multimedia glossary of Catholic Faith Words, Sunday readings, seasonal and Saint resources, and chapter activities go to **aliveinchrist.osv.com**.

Chapter 7 Review

A **Work with Words** Complete each sentence with the correct word from the Word Bank.

1. ___love___ God above all things.

2. The Ten Commandments help you make good ___choices___.

3. The Great Commandment helps you know how to be a good ___neighbor___.

4. ___Share___ what you have with others.

5. ___forgive___ someone who asks you for forgiveness.

B **Check Understanding** Match the Commandment on the left with the correct action on the right.

Column A	Column B
6. You shall not kill.	Say God's name with care
7. Do not take the LORD's name in vain.	Do not harm yourself or others
8. Honor your father and your mother.	Go to Mass on Sunday
9. You shall not steal.	Obey your parents
10. Remember to keep holy the LORD's day.	Do not take what belongs to another

© Our Sunday Visitor

Go to **aliveinchrist.osv.com** for an interactive review.

130 Chapter 7 Review

Choose to Do Good

 Let Us Pray

Leader: Lord, teach us how to make good choices.

"LORD, teach me the way of your statutes;
I shall keep them with care." Psalm 119:33

All: God, help us to follow your laws, with all our
heart. Amen.

God's Word

The servant girl saw Peter and said, "This man is
one of them!" "No, I'm not!" Peter replied. Later, some
of the people said to Peter, "You certainly are one of
them, you're a Galilean!" Once again Peter denied
knowing Jesus. Right away a rooster crowed a second
time. Then Peter remembered that Jesus had told him,
"Before a rooster crows twice, you will say three times
that you don't know me." So Peter started crying.

Based on Mark 14:69–72

What Do You Wonder?

- Why are God's rules or laws important?
- Who helps you make good choices?

A Hard Choice

Why are some choices hard to make?

God made us with **free will**. We are free to choose how we act. Sometimes we make bad choices that do not show love. Peter, one of Jesus' closest friends, had a hard choice to make.

Catholic Faith Words

free will being able to choose whether to obey God or disobey God. God created us with free will because he wants us to make good choices.

God's Word

Peter Denies Jesus

The night before Jesus died on the Cross, soldiers took Jesus away. Peter followed them to a courtyard. The gatekeeper said to Peter, "You are not one of this man's disciples, are you?" He said, "I am not."

Later, Peter was standing around a fire to keep warm. And someone said to him, "You are not one of his disciples, are you?" Peter said, "I am not."

One of the slaves said, "Didn't I see you in the garden with him?" Again, Peter said no.

Based on John 18:17–18, 25–27

Jesus told Peter that he would deny him three times.

Jesus Forgives

Peter did not tell the truth about being Jesus' follower. He did not show his love for Jesus. After Jesus was raised from the dead, he spoke to Peter.

Three times Jesus asked Peter if he loved him. Three times Peter said yes. Jesus believed Peter and asked him to take care of his followers.

Jesus forgave Peter because Peter was sorry for what he had done. Jesus gave us the the Sacrament of Penance so that we could know his forgiveness. If you tell God that you are truly sorry for the wrong you do, he will forgive you.

After his Resurrection, Jesus forgave Peter.

Underline what Jesus did when Peter said he was sorry.

One way we receive God's forgiveness is in the Sacrament of Penance.

Share Your Faith

Think How can you show you are sorry for something?

_____

_____

_____

Share In a small group, talk about ways you respond to someone who tells you they are really sorry.

Choose to Do Good **133**

God Helps You Choose
How do you know right from wrong?

A sin is a person's choice to disobey God on purpose and do what he or she knows is wrong. Accidents and mistakes are not sins.

An accident is something we do not do on purpose. We don't plan accidents or expect them to happen. A mistake is a misunderstanding or an incorrect answer or something we think is right but is not. A sin is a choice to do something we know is wrong. Sin hurts your friendship with God and others.

1. Circle the picture that shows a mistake and put an X over the picture that shows a sin.

2. Discuss what Marita should do next and what Arnie could have done differently.

Marita spilled her milk all over the kitchen counter.

Arnie teased Rachel for losing the game of freeze tag.

Types of Sin

Some choices lead to serious sins called mortal sins. A **mortal sin** is a serious sin that causes a person's relationship with God to be broken. It is a choice to turn completely away from God's love.

A less serious sin is called a **venial sin**. Venial sins hurt a person's relationship with God but do not completely remove him or her from God's life and love. They still matter, though, because they can lead to more serious sins.

God's love is always greater than sin. His mercy never ends.

Conscience

God helps you choose what is good. He gives you a **conscience**. This gift from God helps you know right from wrong. It is important for us to know God's laws so our conscience can help us make good decisions. The Holy Spirit guides you to listen to your conscience.

You know something is right when it follows God's law. You know it is wrong when it goes against one of the Ten Commandments.

Catholic Faith Words

mortal sin a serious sin that causes a person's relationship with God to be broken

venial sin a sin that hurts a person's friendship with God, but does not completely break it

conscience an ability given to us by God that helps us make choices about right and wrong

Connect Your Faith

Identify What are some choices children your age make? Choose one and talk about how God's Commandments can help you know what to do.

Our Catholic Life

How can you make good choices?

When you have to choose, you can remember what you know about being a follower of Jesus. Knowing the difference between right and wrong is not always easy. You can use your conscience, the ability from God to choose what is good and avoid what is not. Here are some steps to follow:

Steps for Making Good Choices

1. Stop what you are doing.

2. Look to what you have learned about the Commandments.

3. Imagine: How can I act like a follower of Jesus right now?

4. Stop and listen to what your conscience is saying, the gift from God to help you know right from wrong.

5. Pray to the Holy Spirit for help.

Next to each picture, write the number of the step that it shows.

People of Faith

Saint Thérèse of Lisieux, 1873–1897

Saint Thérèse of Lisieux lived in France. As a little girl, she sometimes did bad things. She would cry if she didn't get her own way. When her mother died, Thérèse was very sad and decided she would always choose to do what was good. When Thérèse joined the Carmelite convent she said she couldn't do big, important things for God. But she could do little things, like her chores. She offered them to God. She is known as the "Little Flower of Jesus."

October 1

Discuss: What is one little thing you can do for God today?

Learn more about Saint Thérèse at **aliveinchrist.osv.com**

Live Your Faith

Plan a Skit With a partner, write a story about making a choice. Then together act it out.

1. What choice does the person have to make?

_____

2. What things should the person think about before making the choice?

_____

3. What will the person do?

_____

4. Why is it important to think before making a choice to do something?

_____

♥ Let Us Pray

Prayer of Petition

Gather and begin with the Sign of the Cross.

Leader: Our Father, thank you for helping us find the way to life with you and peace with others.

Reader 1: You gave us the Ten Commandments to guide us in our choices.

All: Show us the way, O Lord.

Reader 2: Jesus shows us the way to love and seek forgiveness.

All: Show us the way, O Lord.

Reader 1: The Holy Spirit brings us peace and a forgiving heart.

All: Show us the way, O Lord.

Reader 2: Our family and friends help us choose all that is good.

All: Show us the way, O Lord. Amen.

 Sing "C-H-O-I-C-E-S"

C–H–O–I–C–E–S.
God gives us choices every day.
In every single way (repeat).
© 2008, John Burland. All rights reserved.

FAMILY+FAITH
LIVING AND LEARNING TOGETHER

YOUR CHILD LEARNED >>>

This chapter explains making good choices, the difference between a sin, a mistake, or an accident, and God's willingness to forgive our sin.

God's Word

Read **Mark 14:69–72** to see how Peter denied knowing Jesus after his arrest.

Catholics Believe

- Conscience is the ability given to us by God that helps us make choices about right and wrong.
- Sin is a free choice to do what you know is wrong.

To learn more, go to the *Catechism of the Catholic Church* #1778, 1783–1784 at **usccb.org**.

People of Faith

This week, your child met Saint Thérèse of Lisieux, the Little Flower. She once said she wanted to take an elevator directly to God.

CHILDREN AT THIS AGE >>>

How They Understand Making Good Choices Children need and want limits and guidance. They get a sense of security from structure. But in a society that is increasingly unwilling to make value judgments, children can sometimes be at a loss to know right from wrong. Knowing the rules and understanding how things work are very important to second-graders. Parents, teachers, and catechists serve as important mentors and examples to them. Don't hesitate to tell your child how you feel about various moral issues and choices he or she may face. Children listen to their parents about these things and often internalize a parent's values even when we don't realize it.

CONSIDER THIS >>>

Can you recall a time you received undeserved forgiveness?

That experience leaves us feeling both humbled and grateful. Perhaps that is why we so identify with the people in the Scriptures who experience God's forgiveness. "When Peter asked the number of times a person should forgive, Jesus told him that there should be no limit to forgiving. Jesus forgave Peter his triple denial, showed mercy to the woman taken in adultery, forgave the thief on the cross, and continually witnessed the mercy of God...the Sacrament of Penance is God's gift to us so that any sin committed after Baptism can be forgiven" (*USCCA, p.243*).

LET'S TALK >>>

- Talk about the difference between a mistake and a sin.
- Ask your child to share a story from the Bible that talks about forgiveness. What did that story teach them?

LET'S PRAY >>>

Dear God, help us to do all the "little things" in our lives with love, like Saint Thérèse did. Amen.

For a multimedia glossary of Catholic Faith Words, Sunday readings, seasonal and Saint resources, and chapter activities go to **aliveinchrist.osv.com**.

Chapter 8 Review

A **Work with Words** Fill in the circle beside the correct answer.

1. Your _conscience_ helps you know right from wrong.
   - ○ sin
   - ● conscience

2. _A sin_ ____ is a free choice to do what you know is wrong.
   - ○ An accident
   - ● A sin

3. A _mortal_ sin breaks a person's relationship with God.
   - ● mortal
   - ○ venial

4. A _venial_ sin hurts a person's friendship with God, but does not completely break it.
   - ○ mortal
   - ● venial

5. You must be _sorry_ for your sins before you can ask God's forgiveness.
   - ● sorry
   - ○ scared

B **Check Understanding** The sentences below name the steps for making good choices. Use the numbers 1–5 to put the steps in order.

6. [4] Listen to your conscience.

7. [1] Stop and think.

8. [3] Ask yourself, "What would Jesus tell me to do?"

9. [5] Pray to the Holy Spirit for help.

10. [2] Remember what you have learned about the Commandments.

Go to **aliveinchrist.osv.com** for an interactive review.

God's Mercy

♥ Let Us Pray

Leader: Blessed be our loving God of Mercy.

You, Lord, are a merciful and gracious God, slow to anger, most loving and true.

Based on Psalm 86:15

All: God of mercy and love, bless us and guide us. Amen.

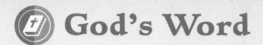

📖 God's Word

"Then Peter approaching asked him, 'Lord, if my brother sins against me, how often must I forgive him? As many as seven times?' Jesus answered, 'I say to you, not seven times but seventy-seven times.'"

Matthew 18:21–22

❓ What Do You Wonder?

- Why does Jesus tell us to forgive?
- How is forgiving others connected to God forgiving us?

Jesus Teaches Forgiveness

When does God forgive us?

Since the time of Adam and Eve, we've all been tempted to do what was wrong and choose sin. The **virtues** are good habits that can help us say no to **temptation**. Even if we fail, and hurt our friendship with God, he is kind and full of **mercy** and always ready to forgive us when we are truly sorry.

 God's Word

The Prodigal Son

Once, a father had two sons. The younger son did not want to stay home. "Give me my half of your money," the son said.

The father sadly gave the younger son the money. The son went to a city far away. He wasted all his money.

The son needed more money, so he got a job feeding pigs. He did not like his job. He was sad and cold and all alone.

He said, "I will go home to my father. I will beg him to give me a job as his servant." The son started to walk home.

One day, the father saw his son far away. The father ran to meet him. The son fell into his arms and cried, "I am sorry I have sinned. I am not good enough to be your son."

The father hugged his son. He threw a big party. The older son said, "That's not fair. He disobeyed you!" But the father said, "He has come home. We must welcome him." Based on Luke 15:11–32

Catholic Faith Words

virtues good habits that make you stronger and help you do what is right and good

temptation wanting to do something we should not, or not doing something we should

mercy kindness and concern for those who are suffering. God has mercy on us even though we are sinners.

⭐ Draw the last part of the story in the empty box.

Share Your Faith

Think Name two people in your life that help you make good choices.

1. _____

2. _____

Share with a partner.

Forgive One Another

How can we forgive others?

God our Father always forgives us if we are truly sorry. He gives us the Sacrament of Penance so we can always have his forgiveness. And Jesus wants us to forgive others in the same way that the Father forgives us!

Read each story and circle who needs to ask for forgiveness. How can they do that? What can the other people in the story say or do to show they forgive?

Sometimes it is not easy to forgive others. You want to stay angry. But, Jesus asks that you make the choice to love the person that hurt you the way that God loves you.

The following stories are about children who made wrong choices.

A New Model

Ethan crept into Michael's room to see his brother's new model airplane. As he picked it up, he broke the wing. Michael walked in and became angry.

Ethan apologized, but Michael screamed, "I will never forgive you!"

"Well, I'll never talk to you again," said Ethan, as he stomped out of the room.

Putting Things Away

Chloe was supposed to put the balls away after recess. She forgot. The next day the balls were gone. Chloe told the teacher that it had been Alex's turn to put the balls away. Alex got in trouble because of Chloe's lie.

Jesus Asks Us to Forgive

Jesus wants you to ask forgiveness when you have done wrong. And Jesus asks you to be a forgiving person, too.

Connect Your Faith

Rewrite the Story Choose one of the stories and write a different ending to show good choices.

_____

_____

_____

_____

God's Mercy   **145**

Our Catholic Life

How do people forgive one another?

When someone has been unkind or unfair, you may be angry with that person. You may not want to talk to him or her. But Jesus asks you to do something very different. Jesus asks you to forgive.

Sometimes you are the person who does the hurting. You need to ask forgiveness if you have been unkind or unfair.

Write one more way you can show forgiveness and one way you can ask forgiveness.

© Our Sunday Visitor

Show Forgiveness

- Be ready and willing to make things better.
- Listen to the person's apology.
- Say "I forgive you," and show it with a hug or a smile.
- Don't hold a grudge or pout.

Ask Forgiveness

- Imagine how it must feel for the other person.
- Say "I'm sorry," and mean it.
- Do whatever you can to make up for the wrong you did.
- Pray to God for help to make better choices.

People of Faith

Saint Jane Frances de Chantal, 1572–1641

Saint Jane Frances de Chantal is one of the few Saints who was a wife and mother. Jane was born in France. As she grew up, her parents helped her to grow in faith. When she was twenty years old, Jane married Christophe. The couple shared their love and their deep faith with their four children. One day, Christophe was killed in a hunting accident. Before he died, he forgave the man who shot him. Jane was heartbroken with grief. She struggled to forgive the man. She prayed to God to help her. Eventually, with God's help, she was able to forgive.

August 12

Discuss: How can you be forgiving?

Learn more about Saint Jane at **aliveinchrist.osv.com**

Live Your Faith

Draw one way someone has shown God's mercy to you.

Think of a way you can show mercy to someone this week.

♥ Let Us Pray

Prayer for Mercy

Gather and begin with the Sign of the Cross.

Leader: For the times when we were slow to forgive those who hurt us,

All: Lord, have mercy.

Leader: For the times when our words and actions have hurt others,

All: Christ, have mercy.

Leader: For the times we have not told the truth,

All: Lord, have mercy.

Leader: May God give us mercy and forgiveness.

All: Amen.

 Sing "God of Mercy"

God of mercy, you are with us.
Fill our hearts with your kindness.
God of patience, strong and gentle,
fill our hearts with your kindness.
Lord, have mercy. Lord, have mercy.
Lord, have mercy upon us.

Repeat

© 1995, 1999, Bernadette Farrell.
Published by OCP. All rights reserved.

FAMILY+FAITH
LIVING AND LEARNING TOGETHER

YOUR CHILD LEARNED >>>

This chapter explains God's mercy and how important it is to show we are sorry and ask for the forgiveness of God and others.

God's Word

 Read **Matthew 18:21–22** to find out how many times Jesus wants us to forgive someone.

Catholics Believe

- God is merciful and forgiving.
- God will always forgive you if you are truly sorry.

To learn more, go to the *Catechism of the Catholic Church* #1428, 1439 at **usccb.org**.

People of Faith

This week, your child met Saint Jane Frances de Chantal, a wife and mother who prayed to God to help her to forgive.

CHILDREN AT THIS AGE >>>

How They Understand God's Mercy God loves us no matter what. A second-grader's understanding of this will be influenced by his or her experience with love and forgiveness from significant adults. It's important that we not overreact to accidents (which are not the same as bad choices unless a bad choice led to the accident). It's also important that when children this age make a purposeful wrong choice, they be given a way to help repair the damage that was done. Finally, be sure to reassure your child of your love, even when he or she makes wrong choices.

CONSIDER THIS >>>

How important is being able to admit you are wrong?

As difficult as it may be to say those words, admitting that we are wrong is the necessary first step in the journey of forgiveness and reconciliation. "God's mercy makes possible the repentance of the sinner and the forgiveness of sin. Time and again in the Old Testament, the sins of the people are met with God's outreach of mercy and the invitation to be healed and return to a covenant relationship" *(USCCA, p. 235).*

LET'S TALK >>>

- Ask your child what Jesus teaches us about forgiveness.
- Talk about a time when you needed forgiveness and received it. Share how it impacted you in some way.

LET'S PRAY >>>

God our Father, help us to be merciful and forgiving like Saint Jane Frances de Chantal. Amen.

For a multimedia glossary of Catholic Faith Words, Sunday readings, seasonal and Saint resources, and chapter activities go to **aliveinchrist.osv.com**.

Chapter 9 Review

A **Work with Words** Complete each sentence with the correct word from the Word Bank.

1. God forgives when we are truly _sorry_.

2. _virtues_ are good habits that help us choose good.

3. We've all been tempted to choose _sin_.

4. God is kind and full of _mercy_.

5. Wanting to do something we should not do is a _temptation_.

B **Check Understanding** Fill in the circle beside the correct answer.

6. You show forgiveness when you listen to a person's ____.
   ○ anger   ◉ apology   ○ stories

7. You need to ask forgiveness if you have been ____.
   ○ unhappy   ○ unloved   ◉ unkind

8. You show forgiveness when you don't hold a ____.
   ◉ grudge   ○ party   ○ sin

9. When you need forgiveness, you can say, "____."
   ◉ I'm sorry   ○ I'm angry   ○ I'm hurt

10. Jesus asks you to ____ those who hurt you.
    ○ hurt   ○ ignore   ◉ forgive

Go to aliveinchrist.osv.com for an interactive review.

A **Work with Words** Find the words in Word Bank in the word search. Circle the word when you find it.

Word Bank

| Commandments | forgives | mortal | love | sin |
| conscience | venial | mercy | accident | Jesus |

1–10.

```
C O M M A N D M E N T S
O A E E C P R Z O S T M
N F S R C Z S L J P R O
S A B C I O P O E A B R
C Q N Y D D Z V S Q C T
I W G T E H R E U M O A
E F Y H N V Z A S Y H L
N Z S M T A O B E D C A
C P I E F C V E N I A L
E X N Y F O R G I V E S
```

B **Check Understanding** Draw a line from each item in Column A to match the correct ending in Column B.

Column A

Column B

11. Jesus teaches that all people are

the way you want to be treated.

12. The Great Commandment tells you to treat others

is in need.

13. Jesus' New Commandment says, "Love one another as

your neighbors.

14. A neighbor can be someone who helps or

the ability God gave you to make choices about right and wrong.

15. Your conscience is

I have loved you."

Draw a line from each item in Column A to match the correct ending in Column B.

Column A

Column B

16. To make a good choice, you must

asks you to forgive.

17. When someone has been unkind or unfair, Jesus

that loving God means loving our neighbor.

18. To ask forgiveness, you should

listen to your conscience.

19. To help you make better choices, you can always

pray.

20. Jesus told a parable to teach his followers

do all you can to help make up for the wrong you did.

C **Make Connections** Write the word or name that best answers the question.

21. I am the ability given to you by God that helps you make choices. What am I?

_____

22. I am the kind stranger who helped the injured man in one of Jesus' parables? Who am I?

_____

23. I denied knowing Jesus three times but he forgave me and asked me to take care of his followers. Who am I?

_____

24. I returned home and my father forgave me for spending his money in one of Jesus' parables. Who am I?

_____

25. I will always forgive those who are truly sorry. Who am I?

_____

The Church

Our Catholic Tradition

- God shares his life with the Church. Grace is sharing in God's life. (CCC, 1997)

- The Seven Sacraments are signs and celebrations of God's life. They give us grace. (CCC, 1131)

- The Seven Sacraments help us celebrate our friendship with Jesus. They help us to follow him. (CCC, 1123)

- The Church year celebrates the Incarnation, life, Death, Resurrection, and Ascension of Jesus. (CCC, 1171)

How does Jesus share his life with us in the Sacraments?

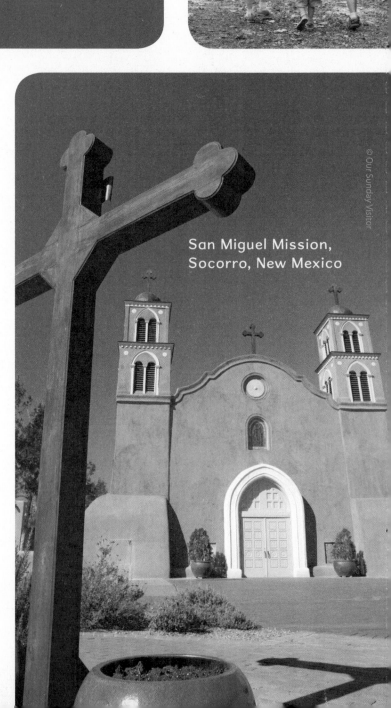

San Miguel Mission, Socorro, New Mexico

© Our Sunday Visitor

The Sacraments

Let Us Pray

Leader: God, thank you for the blessings you give us.

"Come and see the works of God,
awesome in deeds before the
children of Adam." **Psalm 66:5**

All: Help us to see your gifts and fill our
hearts with thanks. Amen.

God's Word

Jesus and his disciples were approaching a town called Jericho. A blind beggar was sitting by the road. When he heard the crowd, he began to shout, "Jesus, Son of David, have pity on me!" People told him to be quiet, but he shouted louder. Jesus stopped and asked that the beggar be brought to him. "What do you want me to do for you," Jesus asked? The blind man said, "Lord, please let me see." Jesus said, "Have sight; your faith has saved you." Immediately the blind man got back his sight and followed Jesus. And the people praised God.

Based on Luke 18:35–43

What Do You Wonder?

- Why did Jesus heal the sick?
- Why do we celebrate the Seven Sacraments?

The Apostles gathering on the mountain where Christ sends them out to share the Good News and baptize in his name.

Signs of God's Love

What are the Sacraments?

Jesus' actions were signs of love that brought people closer to God the Father. Jesus welcomed people who felt alone. He fed people who were hungry. Jesus forgave and healed people. In these ways, Jesus shared God's life with others. Later, the Holy Spirit gave the Apostles the power to do what Jesus had done.

God's Word

The Commissioning of the Apostles

After his Resurrection, Jesus asked his Apostles to continue his work. "Go, therefore, and make disciples of all nations, baptizing them in the name of the Father, and of the Son, and of the holy Spirit, teaching them to observe all that I have commanded you." Matthew 28:19–20

➤ What did Jesus ask the Apostles to do?
➤ Who has taught you about Jesus?

Signs and Celebrations

The Catholic Church shares God's life and love through special celebrations called Sacraments. The **Seven Sacraments** are special signs and celebrations that come from Jesus and allow us to share in God's life.

Baptism is the first Sacrament a person receives. Through Baptism, a person receives forgiveness and new life in Christ. He or she becomes a child of God and a member of Christ's Body, the Church.

In Baptism, a priest or deacon pours water over the head of the person being baptized and says, "I baptize you in the name of the Father, and of the Son, and of the Holy Spirit." The person is then anointed with oil and marked forever by God's love. Afterward, he or she receives a lit candle as a sign of walking in the light of Jesus.

Catholic Faith Words

Seven Sacraments special signs and celebrations that Jesus gave his Church. They allow us to share in God's life and work.

Baptism the Sacrament in which a person is immersed in water or has water poured on him or her. Baptism takes away Original Sin and all personal sin, and makes a person a child of God and member of the Church.

Share Your Faith

Think What is one way girls and boys your age can walk in the light of Jesus?

_____

_____

_____

_____

Share Take turns talking with a partner.

The Seven Sacraments

How do we become Church members?

In the Seven Sacraments, we receive the gift of God's life and help. This is called **grace**. Jesus is present in the Sacraments. He welcomes, heals, and feeds us.

In each Sacrament, the Holy Spirit does things that we can't see. But we are invited to cooperate with his work. We do this by things we can see: our words and actions in the celebration. When you receive the Sacraments, God's life in you grows. You grow in love for him and others.

Baptism, Confirmation, and Eucharist are the **Sacraments of Initiation**. *Initiation* means "beginning." These Sacraments welcome new members into the Catholic Church. Everyone is invited to follow Jesus and join the Church.

Catholic Faith Words

grace God's gift of a share in his life and help

Sacraments of Initiation the three Sacraments that celebrate membership in the Catholic Church: Baptism, Confirmation, and Eucharist

1. Circle the Sacraments you have already received.

2. Draw a square around the ones you will receive soon.

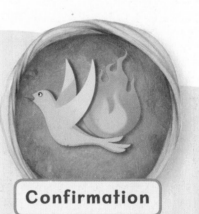

Confirmation

Baptism

Eucharist

The Sacraments of Initiation

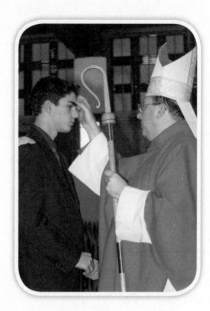

- Through **Baptism**, a person is given new life in Christ.

- In **Confirmation**, a person is sealed with the Gifts of the Holy Spirit and strengthened to follow Jesus.

- In the **Eucharist**, the Body and Blood of Christ help disciples grow closer to him and others.

People of any age can become members of the Catholic Church. Sometimes all three Sacraments of Initiation are received in the same celebration. Other times, they are spread over many years.

Connect Your Faith

Make a Card Create a welcome message for a new Church member. Tell him or her something you think new Catholics need to know about the Sacraments and the Church.

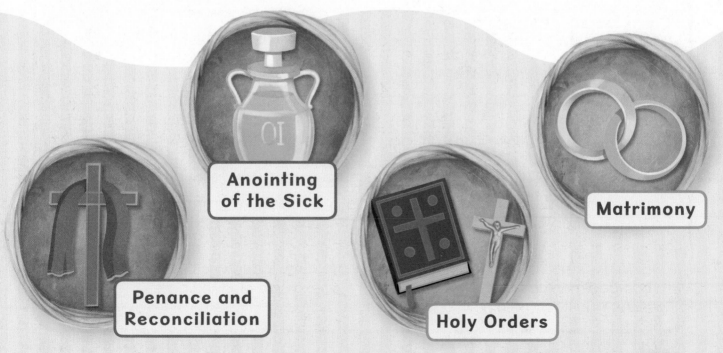

Anointing of the Sick

Penance and Reconciliation

Holy Orders

Matrimony

Our Catholic Life

How do the Sacraments help the Church?

Each of the Sacraments is a sign and a celebration. In the Sacraments, you receive grace. God's life and love help you be more loving. The grace of the Sacraments helps the whole Church community, too.

Match the first three Sacraments on the left to how they help the Church on the right.

What It Celebrates	How It Helps the Church
Baptism Becoming children of God and members of the Church	Feeds, heals, and unites the members of the Body of Christ
Confirmation Being sealed with the Gift of the Holy Spirit	Welcomes new members into the Catholic family
Eucharist Jesus' sacrifice and the gift of his Body and Blood received in Holy Communion	Gives members the strength to follow Jesus' example
Penance and Reconciliation God's forgiveness when we are sorry for and confess our sins	Brings people back into the Church and helps make peace
Anointing of the Sick God's healing love through prayer and anointing with oil	Gives support to people who are ill or elderly
Holy Orders The call of a man to be a deacon, priest, or bishop	Strengthens men to be leaders and to serve God and the Church
Matrimony The lifelong love of a baptized man and a baptized woman who become a new family	Builds family love and gives an example of loving care

People of Faith

Saint Pius X (Giuseppe Sarto), 1835–1914

Giuseppe Sarto was born in Italy. He became a priest and a teacher. He loved children and wanted everyone to learn about Jesus and the Church. When he became Pope, he took the name Pius X. He did many things to show how important the Eucharist is. He encouraged Catholics to receive Holy Communion every day, even children. He knew the Sacraments help us stay close to God.

August 21

Discuss: When do you feel close to Jesus?

 Learn more about Pius X at **aliveinchrist.osv.com**

Live Your Faith

Tell what is happening in the picture.

Draw one way you can make someone feel welcome and see God's love.

161

♥ Let Us Pray

Remembering Baptism

Gather and begin with the Sign of the Cross.

Leader: Let us remember that we are God's children. We share in his life. We are disciples of Jesus.

Reader 1: Jesus sent his Apostles out to make disciples of others, to baptize them and teach them.

Reader 2: Paul wrote: You have been baptized. It does not matter who you are or where you come from. Baptism makes you a disciple of Jesus.   Based on Galatians 3:27–28

Leader: When we were baptized, we were marked with the Sign of the Cross. Listen to what was said.

"Dear children, the Church of God receives you with great joy. In her name I sign you with the Sign of the Cross of Christ our Savior…"
The Order of Baptism of Children, 264

Child: Come forward when your name is called. Dip the fingers of your right hand in the water and bless yourself with the Sign of the Cross.

▶ **All:** Sing "The Seven Sacraments"

The Sacraments, the Seven Sacraments. Signs that come from Jesus and give us grace.

The Sacraments, the Seven Sacraments. Signs that God is with us in a special way.
© 2008, John Burland. All Rights Reserved.

FAMILY+FAITH
LIVING AND LEARNING TOGETHER

YOUR CHILD LEARNED >>>

This chapter explains that Jesus shares his life with us in the Seven Sacraments. He welcomes, feeds, and heals us.

God's Word

 Read **Luke 18:35–43** to learn about a man Jesus healed and how it changed the man's life.

Catholics Believe

- Grace is a share in God's life and help.
- Sacraments are special signs and celebrations that come from Jesus and give grace.

To learn more, go to the *Catechism of the Catholic Church* #1145–1152 at **usccb.org**.

People of Faith

This week, your child met Saint Pius X. He was elected Pope in 1903 and is sometimes called "The Pope of the Eucharist."

CHILDREN AT THIS AGE >>>

How They Understand the Sacraments It's a mystery to us, adults and children alike, that God invites us to communicate with him in his work. The Seven Sacraments have human actions and divine actions—the things people say and do and what God does through the Sacrament.

Your child might tend to only focus on the human actions—the things he or she can see. It's important that we direct children to the ways in which these visible signs help us understand the invisible reality—what God is doing in the Sacrament.

CONSIDER THIS >>>

Have you been a little overwhelmed lately? Do things sometimes seem out of control?

As Catholics, "we recognize that many times in many ways God's special love is such that he offers us help to live in a way that leads to sharing his life... we face a struggle prompted by our culture's understanding that everything is within our human power." Learning to rely on God's grace changes our lives (*USCCA, p. 329*).

LET'S TALK >>>

- Ask your child to name the first Sacrament we receive (Baptism).
- Share about your child's Baptism and how it was special.

LET'S PRAY >>>

 Saint Pius X, pray to God for us that we may receive Jesus in Holy Communion with reverence. Amen.

For a multimedia glossary of Catholic Faith Words, Sunday readings, seasonal and Saint resources, and chapter activities go to **aliveinchrist.osv.com**.

Chapter 10 Review

 A **Work with Words** Complete each sentence with the correct word or words from the Word Bank.

1. Baptism and Eucharist are Sacraments

   of __Initiation_____.

2. During __Baptism_____

   water is poured over the person's head.

3. In Confirmation, you are made stronger

   by the __holy_____spirit_____.

4. Sharing in God's life is called ____grace_____.

5. Each Sacrament is a sign of God's ____love_____.

6. Jesus is present in the ____Sacraments_____.

B **Check Understanding** Fill in the circle beside the correct answer.

7. The Seven Sacraments are ____.
   - ● holy signs
   - ○ holy days

8. ____ people are invited to follow Jesus and join the Church.
   - ● All
   - ○ Some

9. Jesus sent his Apostles out to ____ and baptize.
   - ○ eat
   - ● teach

10. At Baptism, a ____ is given to show the light of Jesus.
    - ○ white garment
    - ● candle

 Go to **aliveinchrist.osv.com** for an interactive review.

Seek Forgiveness

 Let Us Pray

Leader: God, we thank you for
your love and forgiveness.

You have forgiven your people's sins
and all their wrongs. **Based on Psalm 85:3**

All: Thank you, God, for your forgiveness.
Amen.

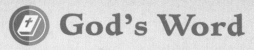 **God's Word**

After Jesus rose from the dead, he went to the disciples who were locked in a room because they were afraid. "Peace be with you," he said. "Whose sins you forgive are forgiven them…" **Based on John 20:21, 23**

© Our Sunday Visitor

? What Do You Wonder?

• Do you think about what your actions say to others?

• Why is forgiveness so important to Jesus?

Making Things Right
How can you show you are sorry?

Sometimes we make choices that accidently hurt someone. Other times, we hurt others on purpose; we choose to sin. In this story, Jesus tells us how to show we are sorry and seek forgiveness.

Underline what Jesus said to the woman after she washed his feet.

🔲 God's Word

The Woman Who Was Forgiven

One day, Jesus was having dinner. An uninvited woman came into the room and knelt at Jesus' feet. She was sorry for her sins. Her tears fell on Jesus' feet. Then she dried his feet with her long hair and poured sweet-smelling ointment on his feet.

Jesus spoke up for the woman. "She has bathed [my feet] with her tears and. . . anointed my feet with ointment. So I tell you, her many sins have been forgiven; hence, she has shown great love."

Then Jesus said to the woman, "Your sins are forgiven. . .Your faith has saved you; go in peace." Based on Luke 7:36–39, 44–50

➡ How did the woman show she was sorry for her sins?

Examination of Conscience

You may sometimes choose not to obey God's laws. This hurts your friendship with God and others.

You can ask the Holy Spirit to help you see where you have made wrong choices. You can think about your thoughts, words, and actions. This prayerful way of looking at your life is called an **examination of conscience**. It helps us know whether what we've done is right or wrong.

Here are some questions you can think about to help you examine your conscience:

- Did I put God first in my life?

- Did I use God's name in a holy way?

- Did I keep Sunday a holy day?

- Did I obey my parents and teachers?

After you think about your sins, you can tell God that you are sorry. Then tell him you will try harder to live by his Commandments. This means you have **contrition** for your sins.

Catholic Faith Words

examination of conscience a prayerful way of thinking about how we have followed the Ten Commandments, Beatitudes, and Church teachings

contrition being sorry for your sins and wanting to live better

Share Your Faith

Think Write one more question you can use to examine your conscience.

_____

_____

Share Share your answer with a partner.

The Sacrament of Reconciliation

How do we receive God's forgiveness?

After examining your conscience and being sorry for your sins, you are ready to celebrate the Church's **Sacrament of Penance and Reconciliation**. Each time you receive this Sacrament, you receive God's forgiveness and celebrate your friendship with him and the Church community.

You can participate in this Sacrament individually or as part of a parish celebration. Either way, you always confess your sins privately to a priest, who grants forgiveness in God's name. The priest will help you if you forget a step.

Catholic Faith Words

Sacrament of Penance and Reconciliation the Sacrament in which God's forgiveness for sin is given through the Church

confession telling your sins to the priest

penance a prayer or an act to make up for sin

absolution words spoken by the priest during the Sacrament of Penance and Reconciliation to grant forgiveness of sins in God's name

Connect Your Faith

Unscramble the Words Find a phrase used during the Sacrament of Reconciliation.

SIH REYCM RNDEEUS OEFRVRE

Steps in the Sacrament

1 **Welcome Rites** The priest greets you with the Sign of the Cross.

2 **Scripture Reading** Sometimes the priest reads, or you quietly read, a Bible passage about forgiveness.

3 **Confession and Penance** Next you tell your sins to the priest. This is called **confession**. He can never tell anyone your sins. He talks with you about ways you can do better. He gives you a **penance**.

4 **Contrition** You pray an Act of Contrition. (See page 170 for this prayer.)

5 **Absolution** The priest gives **absolution**, or forgiveness of your sins, in the name of the Father, the Son, and the Holy Spirit. (See page 315 for the words of this prayer.)

6 **Closing** The priest prays, "Give thanks to the Lord, for he is good." You say, "His mercy endures for ever." You go out to do better and to make up for what you have done wrong.

Our Catholic Life

How do you tell God you are sorry for sin?

In the Sacrament of Reconciliation, you pray an Act of Contrition. This prayer tells God that you are sorry for what you've done and that you need him to help you do better in the future.

Act of Contrition

Match the words of the prayer on the left with what they mean on the right.

Words of the Prayer

My God, I am sorry for my sins with all my heart.

In choosing to do wrong and failing to do good.

I have sinned against you, whom I should love above all things.

I firmly intend, with your help, to do penance,

to sin no more, and to avoid whatever leads me to sin.

Our Savior Jesus Christ suffered and died for us.

In his name, my God, have mercy.

What They Mean

Sometimes I have done wrong things on purpose. Sometimes I haven't done good things that I should have done.

God I know I have done wrong, and I am very sorry.

God, you have asked me to love you with my whole heart, soul, mind, and strength, and I haven't done that.

Jesus died on the Cross to save us from the power of sin.

I believe what Jesus taught us about you, his loving Father. Please forgive me.

From now on, I will try harder to make better choices. I will stay away from people and things that lead me from you.

God, I promise to do the actions and say the prayers that the priest gives me. I need your help.

People of Faith

Saint Benedict-Joseph Labré, 1748–1783

Saint Benedict-Joseph Labré wanted to be a priest, but he had a mental disease and couldn't go to a seminary. Instead, he became a beggar. From the time he was very young, Saint Benedict-Joseph confessed all of the wrong things he did. He would ask God to forgive him. Then he would promise God he would try very hard not to do anything wrong again. Sometimes people were afraid of Saint Benedict-Joseph because he wore rags and lived outside. After he died, people realized that he was a very holy man.

April 16

Discuss: How can you try harder to follow God's laws?

 Learn more about Saint Benedict at **aliveinchrist.osv.com**

Live Your Faith

Tell what is happening in the picture.

Draw one way that you can show you're sorry.

Let Us Pray

Prayer for Forgiveness

Gather and begin with the Sign of the Cross.

Leader: When we don't put God first in our lives,

All: Lord, have mercy.

Leader: When we choose not to obey our parents or teachers,

All: Christ, have mercy.

Leader: When we say or do something to hurt others on purpose,

All: Lord, have mercy.

Leader: When we take something that is not ours,

All: Christ, have mercy.

Leader: When we do not tell the truth,

All: Lord, have mercy.

Leader: Loving Lord, forgive us. Bring us back to you.

All: Amen.

Share a sign of peace.

Sing "Through My Fault"
Through my fault, I choose
what's wrong. Through my fault,
your will's not done.
So, Lord, have mercy be with me.
Christ, have mercy forgive me.
© 2011. John Burland. All Rights Reserved.

FAMILY+FAITH
LIVING AND LEARNING TOGETHER

YOUR CHILD LEARNED >>>

This chapter explains how we celebrate the Sacrament of Penance and Reconciliation and how forgiveness heals people and relationships with God and the Church.

God's Word

 Read **Luke 7:36–39, 44–50** to learn more about how Jesus invites us to look at how we forgive.

Catholics Believe

- In the Sacrament of Penance and Reconciliation, you receive God's forgiveness.
- This Sacrament also celebrates your friendship with God and the Church.

To learn more, go to the *Catechism of the Catholic Church* #1422–1424 at **usccb.org**.

People of Faith

This week, your child met Saint Benedict-Joseph Labré, a homeless beggar who was a very holy man.

CHILDREN AT THIS AGE >>>

How They Understand the Sacrament of Reconciliation
Children at this age might feel nervous about confessing their sins to a priest. They might worry about what the priest will think of them. Tell them that the priest has likely heard every sin confessed and cannot talk to anyone about their confession. The priest is a visible sign of both Christ and the Church, and confession to a priest gives us a chance to experience God's forgiveness in a way that we can see. It's also helpful for children to see a parent receive this Sacrament.

CONSIDER THIS >>>

What makes you believe that someone is truly sorry?

How easy it is to tell "imperfect sorrow" when you have to direct your child to tell his sister he is sorry! In our adult lives it takes great trust to believe that who hurt you is truly sorry. "Contrition that arises from the love of God above all else is called 'perfect contrition.' This loving sorrow remits [forgives] venial sins and even mortal sins so long as we resolve to confess them as soon as possible. When other motives, such as the ugliness of sin or fear of damnation, bring us to confession, this is called 'imperfect contrition,' which is sufficient for forgiveness in the Sacrament" (*USCCA, p. 237–238*).

LET'S TALK >>>

- Ask your child to describe what happens in the Sacrament of Penance and Reconciliation (confession, penance, contrition, and absolution).
- Talk about ways your family asks for and gives forgiveness.

LET'S PRAY >>>

 Dear God, we are sorry for all that we have done wrong, and with your help, we promise to do better in the future. Saint Benedict-Joseph Labré, pray for us. Amen.

For a multimedia glossary of Catholic Faith Words, Sunday readings, seasonal and Saint resources, and chapter activities go to **aliveinchrist.osv.com**.

Chapter 11 Review

 A **Work with Words** Complete each sentence with the correct word from the Word Bank.

1. _____ are the words spoken by the priest during the Sacrament of Penance to grant forgiveness of sins in God's name.

2. In the Sacrament of _____, forgiveness for sin is given through the Church.

3. A _____ is a prayer or an act to make up for sin.

4. The Sacrament of Penance celebrates God's

_____.

 B **Check Understanding** Put the steps of the Sacrament of Reconciliation in order using numbers 1 through 6.

5. Step ☐ The priest forgives my sins in the name of the Father, the Son, and the Holy Spirit.

6. Step ☐ I read or listen to a story of forgiveness.

7. Step ☐ The priest greets me with the Sign of the Cross.

8. Step ☐ I try to do better and make up for my sins.

9. Step ☐ I pray an Act of Contrition.

10. Step ☐ I confess to the priest and receive a penance.

 Go to **aliveinchrist.osv.com** for an interactive review.

The Church Year

 Let Us Pray

Leader: Giving Father, we thank you every day
for all that you give us.

"I will praise you, LORD, with all my heart;
I will declare all your wondrous deeds.
I will delight and rejoice in you;
I will sing hymns to your name, Most
High." Psalm 9:2–3

All: We praise you, Almighty God,
forever and ever. Amen.

 **God's Word**

"Each year his parents went to Jerusalem for the feast of Passover, and when he was twelve years old, they went up according to festival custom." Luke 2:41–42

? What Do You Wonder?

- Why do we celebrate the same things every year?
- What's the most important celebration in the Church year?

Celebrate the Seasons

What seasons are celebrated in the Church year?

During the Church year the **liturgy**, or public prayer, celebrates the events in the life of Jesus. In her **worship**, the Church praises God and celebrates the light of Jesus throughout the Church year.

Advent

During the four weeks of Advent, the Church gets ready to celebrate Jesus' birth. You tell God that you want to get better at loving him and others. Just as the seasons of the year have different colors, so do the Church's seasons. The color for Advent is violet. It is a sign of getting ready and change of heart.

Catholic Faith Words

liturgy the public prayer of the Church. It includes the Sacraments and forms of daily prayer.

worship to adore and praise God, especially in the liturgy and in prayer

© Our Sunday Visitor

Children celebrate the feast of Epiphany by dressing up as Mary, Joseph, and the three wise men.

Christmas

The three weeks of the Christmas season celebrate Jesus' presence in the world. The Son of God came so all people could know his Father's love. The Christmas celebrations help people love Jesus and other people more. White or gold are the colors for the Christmas season. They are a sign of great joy.

Ordinary Time

Ordinary Time comes twice during the Church year. The first time comes after the Christmas season. The second is after the Easter season. During these times, you learn more about Jesus and grow as his follower. Green is the season's color because it is the color of growth.

Underline what the Church celebrates during Christmas.

The lily is a sign of joy, hope, and life. It reminds us of how we grow in Christ.

Share Your Faith

Think What season is the Church in now? Write one way you will celebrate this season.

_____

_____

_____

Share Talk about your answer with a partner.

Volunteers show their love for God and neighbors by helping others during Lent.

Celebrating Jesus

What is the greatest feast of the year?

Lent

The Season of Lent is a preparation for the important feast of Easter. For forty days and six Sundays, the Church's color is violet. As during Advent, you are asked to make changes that will help you grow closer to Jesus. It's a special time to show God you are sorry and fully focused on him. You are to pray more often and help others.

The Three Days

The three days before Easter are the holiest days of the Church year. On Holy Thursday, the Church celebrates Jesus' gift of the Eucharist at the Last Supper. It is a happy occasion, a time of joy, so the color is white.

On Good Friday, the Church gives thanks to Jesus as Savior. The color is red because Jesus died for all people. Holy Saturday evening begins the Easter celebration. For this joyous feast, the color is white.

Easter

Every Sunday, the Church celebrates the **Resurrection**, when Jesus was raised from the dead. But each year, the Church also celebrates the Resurrection of Jesus for fifty days from Easter to Pentecost. Easter is the greatest feast of the Church year. The color during this season is white.

The last ten days of this season celebrate Jesus' promise to send the Holy Spirit. Pentecost is the celebration of the Holy Spirit coming to the Apostles, Mary, and other disciples. For this feast, the color red is used as a sign of the power of the Holy Spirit.

➡ **Why do you think Easter is the greatest feast of the Church year?**

© Our Sunday Visitor

Connect Your Faith

Decorate the Cross and color in the word above it.

Our Catholic Life

How do you know what Church season it is?

Your parish family uses colors to celebrate the Church's seasons and feasts, too. Here are some places you may see colors of the season used in your parish church.

Fill in the blanks to describe the words on the left.

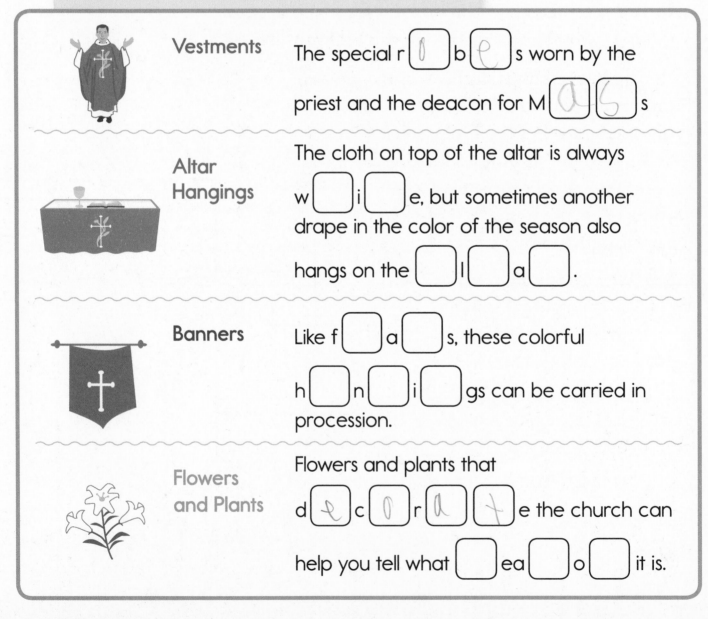

Vestments — The special r[o]b[e]s worn by the priest and the deacon for M[a][s]s

Altar Hangings — The cloth on top of the altar is always w[ ]i[ ]e, but sometimes another drape in the color of the season also hangs on the [ ]l[ ]a[ ].

Banners — Like f[ ]a[ ]s, these colorful h[ ]n[ ]i[ ]gs can be carried in procession.

Flowers and Plants — Flowers and plants that d[e]c[o]r[a][t]e the church can help you tell what [ ]ea[ ]o[ ] it is.

People of Faith

Pope Saint Victor, d. 199

Pope Saint Victor was the first Pope from Africa. When he was Pope, people couldn't agree when to celebrate Easter. They needed to know the day of Easter to plan the seasons of the Church year. Pope Victor and the bishops decided that it must be celebrated on Sunday. He also knew it was important for people to be able to understand the Mass, which was only said in Latin. He declared that the Mass should be said in the language of the people, and today the Mass is said in many languages, including Latin.

July 28

Discuss: What languages have you heard at Mass?

 Learn more about Saint Victor at **aliveinchrist.osv.com**

Live Your Faith

How Do You Celebrate
Choose a Church season and draw how your family celebrates it using the color of the season.

❤ **Let Us Pray**

Bless the God of Seasons

Gather and begin with the Sign of the Cross.

Leader: God our Father, we thank you for all that is beautiful in the world and for the happiness you give us.

Reader 1: We praise you for your daylight and your word which gives light to our minds.

Reader 2: We praise you for our Earth and all the people on it.

All: We know that you are good.
You love us and do great things for us.

 Sing "A Circle of Colors"

It's a circle of colors painting the Church year
with reminders of the love God has for you.
The white and golds of Christmas
and Easter. Pretty purples at
Advent and Lent.
Red at Pentecost and to honor
the Holy Spirit.
Ordinary Time's alive with greens.
Each color chosen for
a special reason.
A circle of colors through
the seasons.

Text and music by Chet A. Chambers.
© 2010 Published by Our Sunday Visitor, Inc.

FAMILY+FAITH
LIVING AND LEARNING TOGETHER

YOUR CHILD LEARNED >>>

This chapter explores how the seasons of the Church year celebrate the life, Death, Resurrection, and Ascension of Jesus.

God's Word

Read **Luke 2:41–42** to see how people listened to what Jesus said.

Catholics Believe

- The Church year celebrates the life, Death, Resurrection, and Ascension of Jesus.
- The Resurrection is the mystery of Jesus being raised from the dead.

To learn more, go to the *Catechism of the Catholic Church* #1188–1195 at **usccb.org**.

People of Faith

This week, your child met Saint Victor. An early Pope, Victor determined that Easter must always be celebrated on a Sunday.

CHILDREN AT THIS AGE >>>

How They Understand the Church Year Children at this age have grown in their awareness of special seasons and times of year. They understand at what time of year they will have a birthday or celebrate Christmas or Easter. They might have missed some of the more subtle indicators of changes in the Church year, like changes in color of vestments and church decor, but can begin to identify them with some help. Point out to your child the times when something has changed in the church to mark a change in the Church year. See if your child can tell you what is different.

CONSIDER THIS >>>

Do you have family traditions in your home that celebrate the Church seasons?

All traditions give children and adults alike a deep sense of continuity and rootedness. Traditions that communicate God's presence in our lives draw us ever closer to God and our Church. "In the Liturgical Year, the Church celebrates the whole mystery of Christ from the Incarnation until the day of Pentecost and the expectation of Christ's second coming...The presence of the Risen Lord and his saving work permeates the entire Liturgical Year: Advent, the Christmas season, Lent, the Easter season, and Ordinary Time" (*USCCA p. 173*).

LET'S TALK >>>

- Ask your child to name one Church season and what we celebrate during that time.
- Share a special childhood memory about a season or feast day, and discuss some ways your family can celebrate the current season.

LET'S PRAY >>>

Saint Victor, help us to always remember the importance of Easter. Amen.

For a multimedia glossary of Catholic Faith Words, Sunday readings, seasonal and Saint resources, and chapter activities go to **aliveinchrist.osv.com**.

Chapter 12 Review

A **Work with Words** Write the letter of the correct season from the Word Bank next to the description of the season.

Word Bank

a. Advent

b. Christmas

c. Lent

d. Ordinary Time

e. Easter

1. ☐ Three weeks of joy that celebrate Jesus' birth and presence in the world.

2. ☐ The season that comes twice during the year.

3. ☐ Four weeks of getting ready to celebrate Jesus' birth and presence with us.

4. ☐ The season that celebrates Jesus' Resurrection.

5. ☐ Forty days of praying and helping others as a way to prepare for Easter.

B **Check Understanding** Write T if the sentence is TRUE. Write F if the sentence is FALSE.

6. ☐ Banners are special robes worn by the priest.

7. ☐ The cloth on top of the altar is white.

8. ☐ Flowers and plants that decorate the church can help you tell what season it is.

9. ☐ The Church's seasons have different colors.

10. ☐ Each year the Church celebrates Pentecost sixty days after Christmas.

Go to **aliveinchrist.osv.com** for an interactive review.

A **Work with Words** Complete each sentence with the correct word from the Word Bank.

1. The _____ is the public prayer of the Church.

2. _____ are special signs and celebrations from Jesus that give us life.

3. _____ is being sorry for sin and wanting to live better.

4. _____ is sharing in the life and work of God.

5. _____ are the words spoken by the priest during the Sacrament of Penance to grant forgiveness of sins in God's name.

Word Bank

Sacraments

grace

liturgy

absolution

contrition

B **Check Understanding** Draw a line from the sentences in Column A to the correct answers in Column B.

Column A	Column B
6. The word Resurrection means	God's forgiveness
7. Pentecost celebrates	Jesus' birth
8. The first Sacrament we receive is	Jesus rose from the dead
9. The Sacrament of Reconciliation gives	the coming of the Holy Spirit
10. Christmas celebrates	Baptism

Write the letter T if the sentence is TRUE. Write the letter F if the sentence is FALSE.

11. ☐ In the Sacraments, you receive grace.

12. ☐ Grace is a share in God's own life and help.

13. ☐ Confirmation is the first Sacrament you receive.

14. ☐ You can only receive the Sacrament of Penance and Reconciliation once.

15. ☐ A priest cannot talk to anyone about your confession.

C **Make Connections** Unscramble the words to complete each sentence.

16. Baptism, Confirmation, and Eucharist are the Sacraments of **IONITATNII**.

_____

17. Thinking about your thoughts, words, and actions is called an examination of **SENOCECINC**.

_____

18. **CAENPEN** is a prayer or an act to make up for sin.

_____

19. Lent is a preparation for the important feast of **RASETE**.

_____

20. During **DRNYOAIR ITME**, you learn more about Jesus.

_____

Describe each of the things used in church during the Church year.

21. Colors: _____

_____

_____

22. Vestments: _____

_____

_____

23. Altar hangings: _____

_____

_____

24. Banners: _____

_____

_____

25. Flowers and plants: _____

_____

_____

Morality

Our Catholic Tradition

- Jesus told us that all are welcome in the Kingdom of God—the world of love, peace, and justice that is in Heaven and is still being built on Earth. (CCC, 543, 2819)

- Jesus taught us to pray to the Father in the Lord's Prayer. (CCC, 2773)

- As Jesus' followers, we share in his life and work. We share the Good News with the world. (CCC, 897, 940)

- We can pray in many ways, for many reasons, at any time. (CCC, 2743)

What do we mean when we pray, "thy kingdom come, thy will be done on earth as it is in heaven"?

Pope Francis teaches and leads us in prayer.

Welcome in the Kingdom

 Let Us Pray

Leader: Lord, we praise you for your love.

"Your mercy to me is great." Psalm 86:13

All: Lord, we praise you for your love. Amen.

God's Word

Some people brought their children for Jesus to bless. But when Jesus' disciples saw them doing this, they told the people to stop bothering Jesus. So Jesus called the children over to him, and said, "Let the children come to me and do not prevent them; for the kingdom of God belongs to such as these...whoever does not accept the kingdom of God like a child will not enter it." Based on Luke 18:15–17

What Do You Wonder?

- How are you like Jesus?
- Where do you share Jesus' love?

© Our Sunday Visitor

Welcomed by Jesus

How did Zacchaeus show his faith in God?

We feel happy when someone invites us to join a group. Being included on a team or in a club makes us feel welcome. By the things he said and did, Jesus showed us that God welcomes everyone.

Catholic Faith Words

faith believing in God and all that he helps us understand about himself. Faith leads us to obey God.

peace when things are calm and people get along with one another

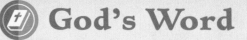 **God's Word**

Zacchaeus the Tax Collector

The news went uphill and down
That Jesus was coming to Jericho town.

Zacchaeus, you know, was too short to see,
So he scurried right up a sycamore tree.

"Zacchaeus, come down, come down, I say.
Let's have dinner at your house today."

Jesus and Zacchaeus walked by the crowd who grumbled and mumbled and said out loud: "He is a sinner and he is a snitch. He took our money. That's why he is rich."

Zacchaeus proclaimed in a loud, clear tone, "To the poor I will give half of all that I own."

Then Jesus said, "God's love has no end. My friend, Zacchaeus, is also God's friend.

Put away your frowns. Be full of cheer. God's love and kindness are truly here.

God calls everyone, the small and the great. So, come gather around. Come celebrate!"

Based on Luke 19:1–10

1. Underline what the mumblers and grumblers said.

2. Circle what Jesus said.

The Surprise Ending

Jesus saw that Zacchaeus had **faith**. Faith is a gift from God, but it's also something we choose. Zacchaeus wanted to follow Jesus. So Jesus surprised everyone. He welcomed Zacchaeus to share in God's love. Jesus wanted him to get along with everyone and be at **peace**.

Share Your Faith

Think Write the name of someone who helps you feel welcome.

_____

Share your answer with a partner.

All Are Invited

Who does Jesus invite to God's Kingdom?

It did not matter to Jesus how old a person was or how tall. Jesus welcomed everyone. Jesus teaches us that people of all ages and backgrounds are welcome in God's Kingdom.

Catholic Faith Words

Kingdom of God the world of love, peace, and justice that is in Heaven and is still being built on Earth

🕮 God's Word

Blessing of the Children

People often brought their children to Jesus. The disciples said, "Don't bother Jesus. He is too busy!" But Jesus said, "Let the children come to me. . .for the Kingdom of heaven belongs to such as these."

Jesus welcomed the children and blessed them. Then he went on his way. Based on Matthew 19:13–15

In God's Kingdom

Another name for the Kingdom of Heaven is the **Kingdom of God**. Jesus invites everyone to enter the Kingdom, to live by God's love and seek his peace. Jesus knew how to make people feel welcome. Many people came to him for help and healing. Some people were like Zacchaeus. They thought Jesus wouldn't care about them. Jesus taught that all people are welcome in God's Kingdom.

Like Jesus, the Catholic Church welcomes all people. In some Catholic parishes there are people who welcome each Church member before Mass begins. These "welcomers" can be men, women, or children. Sometimes these people are called "greeters."

Underline what greeters do.

➔ How do others make you feel welcome?

Connect Your Faith

Fill It In Who does God welcome? Fill in the blanks to complete the statement.

G ☐ D

☐ E ☐ C ☐ M ☐ S

E ☐ E ☐ ☐ O ☐ E

193

Our Catholic Life

What is God's Kingdom like?

Jesus told people about the Kingdom of God. Some people thought Jesus meant a king who lived in a castle. But Jesus was talking about a different kind of Kingdom.

God's Kingdom is filled with joy. Everyone puts God first and works with him to make sure every person has what is needed. By his kindness and care, Jesus showed that everyone is welcome.

God's Kingdom will be complete at the end of time when Jesus returns in glory, but you have already recieved an invitation. When you were baptized, you were welcomed into God's Kingdom.

How are the people in the pictures helping to build God's Kingdom?

People of Faith

Saint Brigid of Kildare, c. 451–525

Saint Brigid was a religious sister who dedicated her life to God. Everywhere Brigid went, she spoke of God's love. She walked and traveled by horse and cart all around Ireland. She sailed in a boat on the Irish Sea. She was known for her kindness and mercy to everyone. She once said that she would like to turn a whole lake into something good to drink and have everyone share it. She wanted everyone to feel loved by God.

February 1

Discuss: How can you share God's kindness and mercy with your friends and family?

 Learn more about Saint Brigid at **aliveinchrist.osv.com**

Live Your Faith

Write an Invitation Fill in the blanks to complete the invitation. Then decorate the invitation with colorful designs.

You Are Invited!

Jesus invites

_____

to the Kingdom of

_____.

Join us this Sunday at

_____.

♥ Let Us Pray

Prayer of Welcome

Gather and begin with the Sign of the Cross.

Leader: God our Father, we gather together in Jesus' name.

Reader 1: When we welcome a friend,

All: Jesus' love shows through us.

Reader 2: When we welcome a child who is left out,

All: Jesus' love shows through us.

Reader 3: When we take extra time to help,

All: Jesus' love shows through us.

Amen.

 All: Sing "Loving Others"

Share the Good News of the Lord and sing.
Shout it out and make the church bells ring!
Show the people on Earth today.
Jesus' love is a better way!

You gotta be good to your neighbor
Good to your friends
Good to your family.
You gotta love one another
Like a sister or a brother
'cause Jesus loves you and me!

© 2010, Nathan Heironimus.
Published by Our Sunday Visitor, Inc.

FAMILY + FAITH
LIVING AND LEARNING TOGETHER

YOUR CHILD LEARNED >>>

This chapter explains Jesus' teaching on the Kingdom and his desire for the Church to welcome and care for all people in his name.

God's Word

Read **Luke 18:15–17** to learn what Jesus says about children in God's Kingdom.

Catholics Believe

- The Kingdom of God is the world of love, peace, and justice that is in Heaven and is still being built on Earth.
- Everyone is welcome in God's Kingdom and in the Catholic Church.

To learn more, go to the *Catechism of the Catholic Church* #543, 544 at **usccb.org**.

People of Faith

This week, your child met Saint Brigid of Kildare. One of the patrons of Ireland, she is known for her kindness and mercy.

CHILDREN AT THIS AGE >>>

How They Understand Caring for Others Our secular society sometimes speaks of the "greater good"—which can mean sacrificing the few for the sake of the many, or violating a smaller principle for the sake of a larger one. Children today are often exposed to this concept. However, our Catholic faith upholds the importance of the common good, the good of everyone, with particular attention to the poor, marginalized, and disadvantaged. Your child will need guidance from you to fully understand this concept and what it means for his or her daily life. A good place to start is in the family, where everyone should be concerned about the good of all.

CONSIDER THIS >>>

How does your family welcome others into your home?

Hospitality is such an important value in the life of a family. When we welcome others into our families, we show love by including and accepting them. In this way the family is an example of the Church. "The Church exists by the will of God the Father and his plan to gather all people under the Lordship of his Son. As Head of the Church, Jesus Christ continues to fill her with his life and saving grace, pouring into her the Holy Spirit with his gifts of unity, peace, and love" (*USCCA, p. 115*).

LET'S TALK >>>

- Ask your child what he or she learned about the Kingdom of God (the world of love, peace, and justice in Heaven and still being built on Earth).
- Together, name some ways to promote peace, fairness, and love in your family.

LET'S PRAY >>>

Saint Brigid, pray for us that we may be welcoming and kind to everyone we know. Amen.

For a multimedia glossary of Catholic Faith Words, Sunday readings, seasonal and Saint resources, and chapter activities go to **aliveinchrist.osv.com**.

Chapter 13 Review

A **Work with Words** Fill in the blank with the correct word or words from the Word Bank.

1. _Zacchaeus_ became Jesus' friend.

2. Jesus _Welcomes_ everyone.

3. Jesus blessed the _children_.

4. Everyone is invited into the _Kingdom of God_.

5. _Faith_ is believing in God and all that he helps us understand about himself.

B **Check Understanding** Fill in the circle beside the correct answer.

6. The Kingdom of God is not about ____.
   - ○ joy
   - ● castles
   - ○ love

7. Jesus showed that everyone is welcome in ____.
   - ○ other countries
   - ○ every club
   - ● God's Kingdom

8. Your ____ welcomes you into God's Kingdom.
   - ○ birthday
   - ● Baptism
   - ○ school

9. God's Kingdom will be ____ at the end of time.
   - ● complete
   - ○ beginning
   - ○ closed

10. At Mass ____ welcome people as they arrive.
    - ● greeters
    - ○ readers
    - ○ singers

 Go to aliveinchrist.osv.com for an interactive review.

198 Chapter 13 Review

Share the Good News

 Let Us Pray

Leader: God, let us sing your songs.

"A psalm of thanksgiving.
Shout joyfully to the LORD, all you
lands." **Psalm 100:1–2**

All: God, fill us with your joy and praise. Amen.

God's Word

Jesus told his disciples: "Go into the whole world
and proclaim the gospel to every creature. Whoever
believes and is baptized will be saved..." **Mark 16:15–16**

? **What Do You Wonder?**

- Why does Jesus ask you to share
the Good News with others?

- How do you share Jesus' Good
News with your family?

Someone Special

When did you have good news to share?

Gaby likes to share stories and pictures of her aunt and uncle. Aunt Jill and Uncle Todd spend a lot of time helping other people. On the weekends they help build houses for families who need a place to live. Last year, they spent their summer vacation in another country providing medical assistance to people who needed it. Gaby wants everyone to know about her aunt and uncle and the special things they do for others.

→ How do you think Gaby shares the news about her aunt and uncle?

Live as Followers

Just like Gaby wants everyone to know about her aunt and uncle, Jesus wanted everyone to know about God his Father.

Catholic Faith Words

Gospel a word that means "Good News." The Gospel message is the Good News of God's Kingdom and his saving love.

Jesus knew that the work of spreading the **Gospel** message about God's Kingdom would be hard. His followers would need his help. He promised to help his followers if they stayed close to him.

➜ **Name one way you can stay close to Jesus.**

🔵 God's Word

The Vine and the Branches

Jesus told his disciples "Remain in me, as I remain in you. Just as a branch cannot bear fruit on its own unless it remains on the vine, so neither can you unless you remain in me."

Jesus said, "I am the vine, you are the branches. Whoever remains in me and I in him will bear much fruit…" John 15:4–5

Zachary

Mrs. Sheperd

⭐ On the leaves, write your name and the names of people you know who are followers of Jesus.

Audrey

Share Your Faith

Think What Good News about Jesus do you want share with others?

Share Talk about these things with a partner.

Taking Jesus' Message to Others

How can we share Jesus' message of love?

The Holy Spirit guided Jesus' followers to places that they had never seen. The Spirit strengthened them to **proclaim** the Gospel. They shared everything that Jesus had taught them with others.

People Who Serve Jesus and Share His Love

Religious sisters and brothers teach children more about God the Father, God the Son, and God the Holy Spirit.

Catechists help children learn songs to sing to God.

Parents and grandparents show their children how to love God.

Jesus' Followers Today

Jesus' followers still bring his message to the world in different ways. There are many people in your **parish**, the place where your local community of Catholics meets, that share Jesus' message. When we share the Good News, we work together with God as he builds his Kingdom.

Priests are pastors who lead the parish, celebrate Mass, and bless people.

Deacons serve in the parish in many ways, including baptizing people.

Catholic Faith Words

proclaim to tell about Jesus in words and actions

parish the local community of Catholics that meets at a particular place

Connect Your Faith

Proclaim the Gospel Name two people in your parish who proclaim the Gospel.

1. _____

2. _____

Our Catholic Life

How can you share the Good News?

Jesus asked all of his followers to share the Good News. He told them to use the gifts God gave them to help them do this. God has given you gifts, too. You have the gifts of time, talent, and treasure to help you share the Good News.

Write in one way you can share your time, talent, and treasure.

Share Your Gifts

Time: All the minutes of your day, which you can choose to use generously or selfishly.

You can: Do extra chores at home or run errands for a neighbor.

_____

Talent: All the things you like to do and things you do well, which you can use generously or selfishly.

You can: Teach someone to play your favorite game or read a story to a younger child.

_____

Treasure: All the things you have, which you could use generously or selfishly.

You can: Let a friend borrow a toy or collect extra clothes and toys for people who have less.

_____

People of Faith

Saint Teresa of Calcutta, 1910–1997

Saint Teresa of Calcutta was born in Albania. She was named Agnes by her parents. When she grew up, she became a nun. Her new name was Mother Teresa. She worked in Calcutta, India, far from her home. She cared for the poor and dying. She began a new group of sisters called the Missionaries of Charity. When people asked, "What can we do to help the people who are poor?" Mother Teresa told them to use their gifts of time, talent, and treasure to build God's Kingdom. She said, "Do something beautiful for God."

September 5

Discuss: How can you do something beautiful for God?

 Learn more about Saint Teresa of Calcutta at **aliveinchrist.osv.com**

Live Your Faith

Share the Good News With a partner, answer the questions about this story.

1. How did the Samaritan use his gifts?

2. What gifts could you use to bring the Good News to someone in need?

♥ Let Us Pray

Prayer of Thanksgiving

Gather and begin with the Sign of the Cross.

Leader: We praise and thank you,
O Lord, for the many people
who share your Good News.
Blessed be the name of the Lord.

All: Now and forever.

Leader: We praise and thank you,
O Lord, for the people
who help in our parish.
Blessed be the name of the Lord.

All: Now and forever. Amen.

Leader: We praise and thank you,
O Lord, for giving gifts and talents
to us to serve others.
Blessed be the name of the Lord.

All: Now and forever. Amen.

 Sing "Gifts"

We thank you, God,
for giving talents to us.
Now we use those gifts to serve others and you.
Singing and teaching, helping each other.
Caring for needs of our sisters and brothers.
We thank you, God,
as we give our talents back to you!

© 2010, Chet A. Chambers.
Published by Our Sunday Visitor, Inc.

FAMILY+FAITH
LIVING AND LEARNING TOGETHER

YOUR CHILD LEARNED >>>

This chapter teaches that we are all called as disciples to share the Good News of Jesus and that priests, deacons, and religious sisters and brothers serve the Church in many ways.

God's Word

Read **Mark 16:15–16** to find out who is saved through Jesus Christ.

Catholics Believe

- Jesus' disciples share in his life and in his work.
- The Holy Spirit helps us proclaim the Gospel in our words and actions.

To learn more, go to the *Catechism of the Catholic Church* #746–747, 900, 904, 905 at **usccb.org**.

People of Faith

This week, your child met Saint Teresa of Calcutta. Her work with others in need reminds us that there are many ways to serve God.

CHILDREN AT THIS AGE >>>

How They Understand Sharing the Good News Children in second grade may think of sharing the Good News of Jesus only as talking about God. While telling others about our faith is an important part of sharing the Gospel, the witness of our lives is the most powerful testimony we can give to our belief in Christ. Second-graders can begin to understand this through the guidance of parents and other teachers as they point out the many choices we make each day, often witnessed by other people. Even when we cannot preach with our words, our actions can say a lot about who we are and what we believe.

CONSIDER THIS >>>

Do you believe that your actions speak louder than your words?

Research tells us that people trust body language more than verbal language. Jesus offered us the perfect image of God, as his words and actions never contradict each other. "We are called, in imitation of the Lord Jesus, to be people who offer ourselves willingly in service to others. Actions of such service can point to Christ's Kingdom of love, justice, mercy, and salvation to all persons, cultures, governments, and other structures of society. We are also called to a life of service to the Church herself" (*USCCA, p. 118*).

LET'S TALK >>>

- Talk about the talents of each member of your family and how they can be used to serve God and share his love with others.
- Name some people in your parish who spread Jesus' message to others.

LET'S PRAY >>>

Dear Jesus, help us use our gifts to do something beautiful for God, as Saint Teresa of Calcutta did. Amen.

For a multimedia glossary of Catholic Faith Words, Sunday readings, seasonal and Saint resources, and chapter activities go to **aliveinchrist.osv.com**.

Chapter 14 Review

A **Work with Words** Fill in the blank with the correct word from the Word Bank to complete each sentence.

1. Jesus said to make ___disciples___ of all nations.

2. The Holy Spirit was sent to help Jesus' disciples ___proclaim___ the Gospel.

3. Jesus told his followers to ___baptize___ all people everywhere.

4. Jesus is the ___vine___, and we are the branches.

5. The gifts of time, ___talent___, and treasure help you share the Good News.

B **Check Understanding** Write the letter T if the sentence is TRUE. Write the letter F if the sentence is FALSE.

6. [T] Jesus told his disciples to proclaim the Gospel.

7. [F] Jesus asked his followers to keep the Good News a secret.

8. [T] God gives us gifts to help us spread the Good News.

9. [T] We work together with God to build his Kingdom.

10. [F] The Holy Spirit strengthened Jesus' followers to proclaim the newspaper.

© Our Sunday Visitor

Go to **aliveinchrist.osv.com** for an interactive review.

208 Chapter 14 Review

Ways to Pray

 Let Us Pray

Leader: Lord, hear us when we pray.

"Gladden the soul of your servant;
   to you, Lord, I lift up my soul." Psalm 86:4

All: Lord, hear us when we pray. Amen.

 **God's Word**

When Jesus had finished praying, one of his disciples said to him, "Lord, teach us how to pray just as John taught his disciples."

So Jesus told them, "When you pray, say: 'Father, hallowed be your name, your kingdom come. Give us each day our daily bread and forgive us our sins as we forgive everyone who has done wrong to us. And keep us from being tempted.'" Based on Luke 11:1–4

? What Do You Wonder?

- Why does Jesus teach us to pray?
- Can you pray by yourself?

Talking with God
What does Jesus teach us about prayer?

When you pray, you talk to and listen to God. The Bible says that Jesus prayed often. He wanted his followers to pray often, too.

Catholic Faith Words

Lord's Prayer the prayer that Jesus taught his disciples to pray to God the Father

Underline what Jesus says about how we are to pray.

God's Word

How to Pray

Jesus said, "When you pray, go to your inner room, close the door, and pray to your Father in secret."

Jesus also told them, "Do not babble like the others, who think that they will be heard because of their many words . . . Your Father knows what you need before you ask him. This is how you are to pray: Our Father in Heaven, hallowed be your name." Based on Matthew 6:5–9

The Lord's Prayer

The name of the prayer that Jesus taught his followers is the **Lord's Prayer**. It is also called the "Our Father." When we say the Lord's Prayer, we are talking directly to God our Father.

Jesus showed us to pray at all times.

The Lord's Prayer

Words of the Prayer	What They Mean
Our Father, who art in heaven, hallowed be thy name;	We praise God the Father. We say his name with love and respect.
thy kingdom come,	We pray that all people will know God's justice and peace.
thy will be done on earth as it is in heaven.	We will do what God wants, not what we want.
Give us this day our daily bread;	We ask God to give us what we need for now.
and forgive us our trespasses as we forgive those who trespass against us;	We ask God to be as forgiving of us as we are of others.
and lead us not into temptation, but deliver us from evil.	We ask God to protect us from harm and keep us from sin.
Amen.	May it be so!

Share Your Faith

Think When do you pray the Lord's Prayer?

_____

_____

_____

Share Talk about the times the Lord's Prayer is prayed.

Types of Prayer

What is your favorite way to pray?

Prayer is a way to deepen your friendship with God. You can pray in many ways. You can say many things when you pray to God. Sometimes you can just be quiet and enjoy being with God. Listed below are different types of prayers.

Catholic Faith Words

blessing a prayer that blesses God, who is the source of everything that is good

petition asking God for what we need

intercession asking God to help others

thanksgiving giving thanks to God for all he has given us

praise giving God honor and thanks because he is God

Color the picture. Then share one thing you pray for before you go to bed.

How to Pray

You can use your words to pray. You can also use prayers that the Church and some of the Saints have written. These prayers include the Hail Mary, the Glory Be, and prayers before meals. You can pray when you are happy, sad, alone, or with others.

You can also pray when you see pictures or objects that remind you that God is with you. Objects such as a crucifix, a rosary, or holy water are called **sacramentals**. Words of blessing and actions, such as the Sign of the Cross, are also sacramentals.

→ **What sacramentals do you see in church?**

→ **What sacramentals do you have in your home?**

Catholic Faith Words

sacramentals blessings, objects, and actions that remind you of God and are made sacred through the prayers of the Church

Connect Your Faith

Learn by Heart Memorize the words of the Glory Be.

Glory be to the Father
and to the Son
and to the Holy Spirit,
as it was in the beginning
is now, and ever shall be
world without end. Amen.

The crucifix is a sacramental that we see often on necklaces, walls, and in processions at church.

Our Catholic Life

How can you talk to God?

Sometimes you talk to God using the words of prayers you have memorized, like the Lord's Prayer. Sometimes you pray in the words of the Bible, like the psalm verses. But you can use your own words, too, when you pray together with your family and by yourself.

➜ **What are some prayers you can pray?**

Fill in the blanks to identify the prayer type.

Prayer Type	Words We Can Say
A prayer of b l e s s i n g	I love you God, your goodness fills the world.
A prayer of p e t i t i o n	I have a problem and I need your help. God, please help me. I need to know you are with me.
A prayer of I n t e r c e s s i o n	God, please help Uncle Mike find a new job.
A prayer of T h a n k s g i v i n g	Thank you, God, for my family and friends, who share your love with me.
A prayer of p r a i s e	God, the world you made is so amazing!

People of Faith

Saint Alphonsus Liguori, 1696–1787

Saint Alphonsus Liguori was a very good lawyer. God wanted him to become a priest, so he did. He was an even better priest than he was a lawyer. Saint Alphonsus loved to pray. He wrote many different prayers. He wrote prayers of praise, thanksgiving, and petition. He especially loved to ask the Blessed Mother to pray for him. He was also a painter, poet, and musician. He even wrote a song to sing at Christmas!

August 1

Discuss: What type of prayer do you like to pray?

 Learn more about Saint Alphonsus Liguori at **aliveinchrist.osv.com**

Live Your Faith

Write a Prayer Write a short prayer of thanksgiving to God. Tell what you are thankful for and why.

_____

_____

_____

_____

_____

_____

Let Us Pray

The Lord's Prayer

Gather and begin with the Sign of the Cross.

Leader: Let us pray together the prayer that Jesus taught us.

All: Our Father, who art in heaven,
hallowed be thy name;
thy kingdom come,
thy will be done
  on earth
as it is in heaven.

Give us this day our daily bread,
and forgive us our trespasses,
as we forgive those who trespass
  against us;
and lead us not into temptation,
but deliver us from evil. Amen.

Sing "Open My Eyes"

Open my eyes, Lord.
Help me to see your face.
Open my eyes, Lord.
Help me to see.

Open my ears, Lord.
Help me to hear your voice.
Open my ears, Lord.
Help me to hear.

Based on Mark 8:22–25. ©1988, 1999, Jesse
Manibusan. Published by spiritandsong.com ®,
a division of OCP. All rights reserved.

FAMILY + FAITH
LIVING AND LEARNING TOGETHER

YOUR CHILD LEARNED >>>

This chapter explores the importance of prayer, the many ways we pray, and how we use sacramentals—sacred objects, actions, and words.

God's Word

Read **Luke 11:1–4** to learn what Jesus taught us about prayer and the words he used to pray.

Catholics Believe

- Prayer is being with God in your mind and heart. We pray in many ways, for many reasons.
- Jesus taught his followers the Lord's Prayer.

To learn more, go to the *Catechism of the Catholic Church* #2692–2696 at **usccb.org**.

People of Faith

This week, your child met Saint Alphonsus Liguori. He loved to pray to the Blessed Mother.

CHILDREN AT THIS AGE >>>

How They Understand Prayer Children may view prayer as "prayers:" memorized, recited words we say to God. These prayers can be important because they allow us to pray together with one voice, but prayer is a conversation with God, in our hearts, minds, and with words. If they haven't already, children in second grade are old enough now to begin speaking to God in their own words. Your child can do this with some prompting and structure. A sacred space in the home can also provide a place for listening to God in quiet reflection.

CONSIDER THIS >>>

Do you remember seeing sacred pictures and objects in the home where you were raised?

We are transformed by images. Whether it is a piece of great art or a picture of a suffering child we see on the news, images can change our minds and hearts. Faith-filled people can come to know the grace that flows from Christ through the use of sacramentals (blessings, objects, and actions that remind you of God and are made sacred through the prayers of the Church). "We use these signs and symbols to help us experience God's invisible presence" (*USCCA, p. 171*).

LET'S TALK >>>

- Invite your child to share one thing Jesus teaches us about prayer.
- Talk about some ways your family prays together and why.

LET'S PRAY >>>

Mary, I kneel here before you with my family and choose you for my Mother (Saint Alphonsus' family prayer of dedication).

For a multimedia glossary of Catholic Faith Words, Sunday readings, seasonal and Saint resources, and chapter activities go to **aliveinchrist.osv.com**.

Chapter 15 Review

 A **Work with Words** Unscramble the words to find five good reasons to pray.

1. To **LEBSS** God the Father   _bless_

2. To **ESIARP** the Lord for his greatness   _praise_

3. To **KNATH** Jesus for his gift of life   _thank_

4. To **KAS** the Holy Spirit for what you need   _ask_

5. To **RPAY** for someone else   _pray_

B **Check Understanding** Draw a line from the prayers in Column A to the best description of that prayer in Column B.

Column A

6. Loving Father, you are the best!

7. I bless you and love you, God.

8. Jesus help me today in school.

9. Please, Lord, help Grandma get well.

10. Thank you, God, for all my friends.

Column B

prayer of thanksgiving

prayer of blessing

prayer of intercession

prayer of praise

prayer of petition

 Go to **aliveinchrist.osv.com** for an interactive review.

A **Work with Words** Complete each sentence with the correct word from the Word Bank.

Word Bank

proclaim

teachings

faith

Kingdom of God

Lord's Prayer

1. To _____ the Good News about Jesus is to tell about him in word and action.

2. Jesus taught us the _____.

3. _____ is believing in God and that he helps us understand about himself.

4. The _____ is in Heaven and is still being built on Earth.

5. Jesus' disciples believed in him and in his _____.

B **Check Understanding** Circle the correct answer.

6. Who did Jesus call from the tree?

   Peter   John   Zacchaeus

7. Who does Jesus invite to the Kingdom of God?

   everyone   Saints   only children

8. Who is always guiding the Church's actions?

   Saints   Holy Spirit   disciples

9. What name do we give to rosaries and holy water?

   Sacraments   prayers   sacramentals

10. When will Jesus be with us?

    always   when we dream   when we sin

Write the letter T if the sentence is TRUE. Write the letter F if the sentence is FALSE.

11. ☐ Peace is when things are not calm and people do not get along.

12. ☐ Intercession is a prayer in which we ask God to help others.

13. ☐ A petition is a prayer in which we give God honor because he is God.

14. ☐ Jesus asked all of his followers to share the Good News.

15. ☐ Sometimes you can use memorized prayers to pray.

C **Make Connections** Circle the word or words below that tell something about God's Kingdom.

16–20.

justice	praying	stealing
ignoring someone	lying	being unfair
peace	love	kindness
sharing your gifts	being selfish	welcome

Complete each sentence below.

21. Jesus saw that Zaccheaus had

_____.

22. God gave you time, talent, and treasure to help you share the

_____.

23. Prayer is a way to deepen your friendship with

_____.

24. Jesus taught that all people are welcomed in God's

_____.

25. When you thank God in a prayer it is called a prayer of

_____.

Sacraments

Our Catholic Tradition

- The Mass is another name for the celebration of the Eucharist. (CCC, 1332)

- The Mass has two parts: the Liturgy of the Word and the Liturgy of the Eucharist. (CCC, 1346)

- At every Mass, we hear God's Word from the Bible and pray for the Church and the needs of the world. (CCC, 1349)

- We remember Jesus' sacrifice and give thanks for it. (CCC, 1350)

- We receive Christ's Body and Blood in Holy Communion. (CCC, 1355)

How is the Mass both a holy meal and a sacrifice?

Gather to Worship

♡ Let Us Pray

Leader: God, we gather to worship with you.

"It is good to give thanks to the LORD…
To proclaim your love at daybreak,
your faithfulness in the night…" Psalm 92:2–3

All: Thank you, God, for being with us
and filling us with your grace. Amen.

📖 God's Word

"And it happened that, while he was with them at table, he took bread, said the blessing, broke it, and gave it to them. With that their eyes were opened and they recognized him, but he vanished from their sight. Then they said to each other, 'Were not our hearts burning [within us] while he spoke to us on the way and opened the scriptures to us?'" Luke 24:30–32

❓ What Do You Wonder?

- Where do you go to be fed by Jesus?
- How does Jesus feed you?

Celebrating the Eucharist

Who gathers for the Mass?

How much do you look forward to your birthday or Christmas? We gather with people we love to celebrate and share these important events.

Celebrations are an important part of Church life, too. The **Eucharist** is the Sacrament in which Jesus shares himself with us and the bread and wine become his Body and Blood. Since the beginning, followers of Jesus have come together to worship.

Underline the things that Jesus' first followers did that your parish community does, too.

God's Word

The Community Gathers

After the Holy Spirit came, Jesus' followers met often to learn from the Apostles, to break bread together, and to pray. Some of the members sold what they had and gave the money to help the others. Still others shared their belongings with those who were in need. These followers of Jesus were very happy, and new members joined every day.

Based on Acts 2:42–47

We Gather

Mass is another name for the celebration of the Eucharist. Every Sunday, people wave and greet each other as they walk toward their church. As we enter the church, we dip our hands in holy water and make the Sign of the Cross. This action reminds us of our Baptism.

All those gathered together make up the **assembly**. We take part in the Mass by praying, singing, and using actions to worship God.

As the Mass begins, the assembly stands. We all sing a gathering song. The altar servers enter carrying a cross in a procession. The readers, deacon, and priest follow. They are singing, too.

Catholic Faith Words

Eucharist the Sacrament in which Jesus shares himself, and the bread and wine become his Body and Blood

Mass the gathering of Catholics to worship God. It includes the Liturgy of the Word and the Liturgy of the Eucharist.

assembly the people gathered together for worship

Share Your Faith

Think Write one way you can get ready to take part in the Mass.

_____

_____

Share Talk about what happens in your home or parish before Mass begins.

The Introductory Rites

What happens as Mass begins?

After the procession ends, the priest leads the assembly in making the Sign of the Cross. He greets everyone, saying, "The Lord be with you." The assembly answers, "And with your spirit." These words remind us that Jesus is present in the priest and in the people gathered together.

Next, the members of the assembly recall God's forgiveness. The priest asks us to think of times we may have hurt others. We ask for God's mercy and for him to forgive us for any wrong we have done during the week. We say together:

> **Priest:** Lord, have mercy.
>
> **All:** Lord, have mercy.
>
> **Priest:** Christ, have mercy.
>
> **All:** Christ, have mercy.
>
> **Priest:** Lord, have mercy.
>
> **All:** Lord, have mercy.

Underline the responses that you say at Mass.

Words of Praise

With God's forgiveness in your heart, you are better able to pray and take part in the Mass. Many times during the year, the *Gloria* is sung or prayed during Mass. The *Gloria* is a very old hymn that the Church prays to give praise and honor the Holy Trinity. The hymn begins with these words.

All: Glory to God in the highest, and on earth peace to people of good will.

After this song, the priest invites the people to pray. The priest and assembly are silent for a few moments. The priest then prays the opening prayer, and the people respond "Amen." The Introductory Rites have ended. All gathered are now ready for the first main part of the Mass.

Connect Your Faith

Unscramble the Words Find the name of the hymn that we sing during Mass.

LRGOY TO ODG IN HTE SEGHITH

Our Catholic Life

How can you take part in the celebration of the Mass?

The priest leads us in the celebration of the Mass. But he is not the only person celebrating. The whole assembly gathers to praise and give thanks to God.

You are part of the assembly. You don't go to Mass to watch but to take part in the celebration. Taking part in the Mass will help you grow closer to Jesus in the Eucharist.

Ways to Join in the Mass

- Get to know the parts of the Mass.

- Learn the prayers and responses.

- Arrive on time and ready to participate.

- Greet and be friendly to the other people in the assembly.

- Join in the singing.

- Follow the actions of the priest, deacon, and other ministers.

- Listen to all of the readings and the homily.

- Show respect in the way you stand, sit, and kneel.

People of Faith

Saint Tarcisius, third or fourth century A.D.

Saint Tarcisius lived in Rome. He loved Jesus very much. One day, he secretly carried the Eucharist to Christians who were jailed because of their faith in Jesus. Some people who were not Christians discovered what he did. They wanted to take the Eucharist from him. They threw stones at him and killed him. When they looked at his robes they saw that the Eucharist had disappeared! Saint Tarcisius reminds us to always respect the Eucharist because it is Jesus.

August 15

Discuss: How can you show respect for Jesus in the Eucharist?

Learn more about Saint Tarcisius at **aliveinchrist.osv.com**

Live Your Faith

Picture Yourself Celebrating Draw yourself taking part in the Mass with your family and with other members of the assembly.

❤ **Let Us Pray**

Prayer of Praise

Gather and begin with the Sign of the Cross.

All: In the name of the Father,

Group 1: the maker of stars and planets, oceans and mountains,

Group 2: who created all living things,

Group 3: who brought us to life and keeps us alive today and all our days.

All: And of the Son,

Group 1: God who became man,

Group 2: who taught us and celebrated with us,

Group 3: who died and rose to save us.

All: And of the Holy Spirit,

Group 1: who guides, strengthens, and helps us,

Group 2: who remains in our hearts,

Group 3: who will be with us to the end.

All: Amen.

▶ Sing "We Glorify You"

God the Father, we praise you.
God the Father, we bless you.
God the Father, we adore you.
God the Father, we glorify you.
Jesus Christ, we praise you…
Holy Spirit, we praise you…

© 2011, John Burland. All rights reserved.

© Our Sunday Visitor

FAMILY+FAITH
LIVING AND LEARNING TOGETHER

YOUR CHILD LEARNED >>>

This chapter is about gathering as the Church at Mass to praise God and how our community takes part in the celebration.

God's Word

Read **Luke 24:30–32** to learn more about longing for Jesus in the Eucharist.

Catholics Believe

• Mass is another name for the celebration of the Eucharist.

• The assembly uses songs, prayers, and actions to worship God.

To learn more, go to the *Catechism of the Catholic Church* #1141–1142 at **usccb.org**.

People of Faith

This week, your child met Saint Tarcisius of Rome, who risked his life and was eventually killed while trying to bring the Eucharist to imprisoned Christians.

CHILDREN AT THIS AGE >>>

How They Understand the Mass Second-graders may see the Mass as primarily an adult activity, but they are preparing to join together with the parish in the Eucharistic celebration on the day of their First Communion. It's important that they are able to really share in the celebration by being familiar with the liturgy and its meaning. They are ready to understand in more detail the parts of the Mass, their meanings, and how to participate fully. A child-friendly missal can assist children in becoming more familiar with the Mass and following along with the prayers, responses, and readings.

CONSIDER THIS >>>

How important is it for you to gather with those you love to celebrate important moments?

There is a reason that the day before Thanksgiving and Christmas are peak travel times. Sitting at the table with those we love feeds our soul. At Mass, we gather in celebration to give thanks and praise for the love of our God. "The Christian community, united by the Holy Spirit, gathers for worship in response to God's call. Jesus, our High Priest, is the principal agent of our celebration" (*USCCA, p. 218*).

LET'S TALK >>>

• Ask your child to explain what happens at the beginning of Mass.

• Talk about ways your family participates in the Mass and can serve in the celebration.

LET'S PRAY >>>

Almighty God, help us be generous in our gifts to the Church. Amen.

For a multimedia glossary of Catholic Faith Words, Sunday readings, seasonal and Saint resources, and chapter activities go to **aliveinchrist.osv.com**.

Chapter 16 Review

A **Work with Words** Circle the correct answer.

1. The ____ is the great celebration of the Church.

   Eucharist   assembly   procession

2. At Mass, the whole ____ gathers to praise God.

   class   assembly   neighborhood

3. The ____ is a very old hymn that the Church prays to give praise and honor to the Holy Trinity.

   Amen   opening prayer   Gloria

4. As Mass begins the assembly sings the ____.

   gathering song   Sign of the Cross   Lord's Prayer

5. Taking part in the Mass helps us grow closer to ____.

   Jesus   the priest   the deacon

B **Check Understanding** Use the numbers 1 to 5 to put the actions in the order they happen at Mass.

6. ☐ The altar servers, readers, deacon, and priest process into the church.

7. ☐ The priest leads us in the Sign of the Cross.

8. ☐ The priest says, "The Lord be with you."

9. ☐ The assembly gathers.

10. ☐ The priest and assembly say, "Lord, have mercy."

 Go to aliveinchrist.osv.com for an interactive review.

Listen to God's Word

♥ Let Us Pray

Leader: Lord, your Word gives us hope.

"I wait for the LORD,
my soul waits
and I hope for his word." Psalm 130:5

All: God, open my ears so I can
better hear your Word. Amen.

📖 God's Word

Jesus said, "What is God's Kingdom like? What can I compare it with? It is like what happens when a woman mixes a tiny little bit of yeast into a batch of flour. The yeast makes the whole batch of dough rise."

Based on Luke 13:18–21

❓ What Do You Wonder?

- How are the stories in the Bible different from other stories?
- Can the Word of God in the Bible really change my heart?

God's Word Proclaimed
What do you hear at Mass?

Jesus learned the stories of the Jewish people. He studied Scripture and talked about God's law with wise teachers. Jesus was a wonderful teacher, too.

He told many parables. Parables are stories about everyday life that Jesus told to help his followers learn how to love and follow God. Jesus wanted everyone to know that the Kingdom would grow with prayer and sharing in God's work of love, peace, and justice. Here is one parable Jesus told.

Catholic Faith Words

Liturgy of the Word the first main part of the Mass during which we hear God's Word proclaimed

📖 God's Word

The Mustard Seed

"The kingdom of heaven is like a mustard seed that a person took and sowed in a field. It is the smallest of all the seeds, yet when full-grown it is the largest of plants. It becomes a large bush, and the 'birds of the sky come and dwell in its branches.'" Matthew 13:31–32

1. Color in the picture.
2. Underline the name of the parable it illustrates.

The Scripture Readings Begin

The first main part of the Mass is the **Liturgy of the Word**. The assembly listens to God's Word from the Bible.

- The reader steps forward to proclaim the first reading. It is usually from the Old Testament.

- Next, a singer, called a cantor, leads everyone in singing a psalm. Remember, psalms are prayers found in the Old Testament.

- Then, either another reader or the same reader stands and reads the second reading from one of the letters in the New Testament.

- At the end of each reading, the reader says, "The word of the Lord." The assembly answers, "Thanks be to God."

After each reading, everyone quietly thinks about what they have heard.

1. Circle the part of the Bible where the first reading comes from.

2. Underline the part of the Bible where the second reading comes from.

Share Your Faith

Think Complete the sentence: "I learn about God's Word by…"

_____

_____

Share Talk about different ways you learn about God's Word.

A deacon crosses his forehead, lips, and chest before reading the Gospel.

Jesus' Good News

What happens after the First and Second Readings?

Catholic Faith Words

homily a short talk about the readings at Mass

creed a statement of the Church's beliefs

Prayer of the Faithful prayer at Mass for the needs of the Church and the world

Now, everyone stands and sings "Alleluia!" It is time to hear the Good News of Jesus Christ.

"The Lord be with you," says the priest or deacon. The assembly immediately replies, "And with your spirit."

The priest or deacon announces what Gospel is going to be read. The Gospels contain stories about Jesus, the words of Jesus, and stories that Jesus told. The priest or deacon reads the Good News of Jesus from one of the Gospels.

At the end of the Gospel, the priest or deacon says, "The Gospel of the Lord." Everyone says, "Praise to you, Lord Jesus Christ."

After the Gospel reading, the priest or deacon gives a **homily**, a short talk about the readings that helps explain what it means to follow Jesus.

The People Speak

The assembly then stands to pray the **creed**. We say proudly that we believe in God the Father, God the Son, and God the Holy Spirit. We say that we believe in the Church and her teachings.

Next, the assembly stands together and prays the **Prayer of the Faithful**.

As a leader says each prayer, we respond with our answer, such as "Lord, hear our prayer."

- We pray for the leaders of the Church and of our country.

- We pray for those who are sick and those who have died.

- We pray for people all around the world who have needs at this time.

Connect Your Faith

Write Prayers Think of things that are happening in your family or in your neighborhood. Fill in the blanks in these prayers.

For _____, we pray to the Lord.

For _____, we pray to the Lord.

Our Catholic Life

How did Jesus use stories to teach?

Jesus was a great storyteller. He used lots of details and characters that were familiar to his listeners. Often his parables had surprise endings to make people think. Jesus' stories taught people about God the Father's love and ways to love God and others. This year you have read some of these parables.

Parables You've Heard

Match the story on the left to the description on the right.

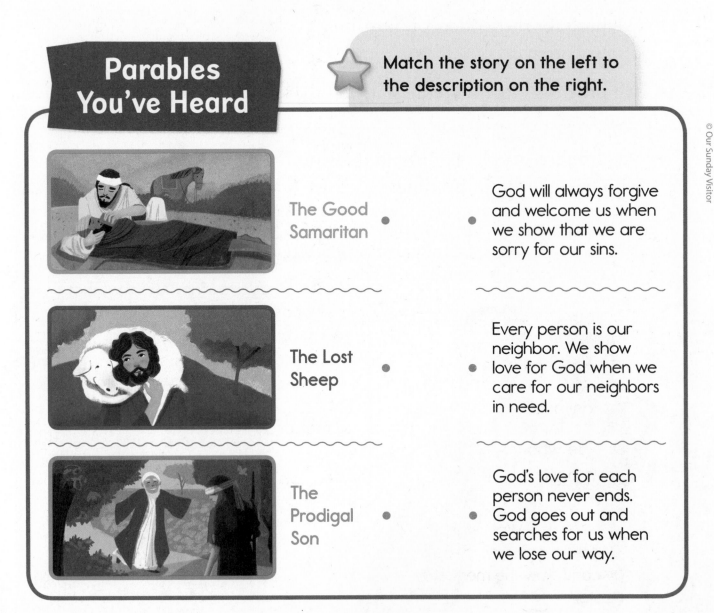

The Good Samaritan

God will always forgive and welcome us when we show that we are sorry for our sins.

The Lost Sheep

Every person is our neighbor. We show love for God when we care for our neighbors in need.

The Prodigal Son

God's love for each person never ends. God goes out and searches for us when we lose our way.

People of Faith

Saint Paul, first century

Saint Paul did not always like Christians. He helped put them in jail. Then one day, Paul heard a voice from above say, "Why do you persecute me?" It was Jesus. Paul realized that he had done wrong. That very minute, Paul stopped hurting Christians. Instead, he went everywhere telling people about Jesus. He started many churches. He traveled and wrote letters to teach about God. He gave people advice on how to love Jesus. Now we read his letters at Mass. They are called "Epistles."

June 29

Discuss: If you were writing a letter about Jesus, what would you write?

Learn more about Saint Paul at **aliveinchrist.osv.com**

Live Your Faith

Act It Out With a small group, choose one of Jesus' parables to act out. Use these steps to help you plan your play.

1. Choose one of Jesus' parables you have heard.

2. Make a list of the people and the animals in the story.

3. Decide who will play each part.

Talk It Over With your group, talk about ways people today can follow the message of this story.

Let Us Pray

Celebration of the Word

Gather and begin with the Sign of the Cross.

Leader: Gracious God, open our hearts and minds to hear your Word.

Reader 1: A reading from the First Letter of John.

Read 1 John 5:13–14.

The Word of the Lord.

All: Thanks be to God.

Sing together the refrain.

Reader 2: A reading from the holy Gospel according to Matthew.

Read Matthew 7:7–8.

The Gospel of the Lord.

All: Praise to you, Lord Jesus Christ.

Say together the Apostles' Creed on page 304.

I believe in God,
the Father almighty,
Creator of heaven and earth,
and in Jesus Christ, his only Son,
our Lord...

 Sing "Gospel Acclamation"

FAMILY + FAITH
LIVING AND LEARNING TOGETHER

YOUR CHILD LEARNED >>>

This chapter focuses on the Liturgy of the Word, the first main part of Mass in which we hear God's Word in the Bible.

God's Word

 Read **Luke 13:18–21** to find out what Jesus said about the Kingdom of God.

Catholics Believe

- In the Liturgy of the Word, God's living Word is read.
- We profess what we believe about God and pray for the needs of the Church and the world.

To learn more, go to the *Catechism of the Catholic Church* #1154, 1349 at **usccb.org**.

People of Faith

In this chapter, your child met the great Apostle, Saint Paul. He wrote many letters that are part of the New Testament.

CHILDREN AT THIS AGE >>>

How They Understand the Liturgy of the Word Second-graders might not have yet picked up the connection between the Lectionary readings in Mass. Paying attention to the relationship between each Sunday's passages from the Old Testament, Psalms, New Testament, and Gospel will help your child's overall understanding of the Scriptures and will encourage more active participation in the Mass. Some discussion about the readings prior to Mass can help to facilitate this. The readings for each Sunday can be found on the U.S. Bishops' site at **usccb.org/nab**.

CONSIDER THIS >>>

Do you long to hear God's voice?

Longing for God's presence is part of our human experience. Our desire for God is written in our hearts, because man is created by God and for God. "Every human person seeks to know the truth and to experience goodness. Moral goodness appeals to us.... The more we become aware of these truths, the more we are drawn to the reality of God who is the Supreme Good. These are the seeds of eternity within us that have their origins only in God" (*USCCA, p. 4*).

LET'S TALK >>>

- Ask your child to describe what happens in the Liturgy of the Word, the first main part of the Mass (readings, homily, creed, Prayer of the Faithful).
- Talk about times you have read the Bible as a family or when you were a child or adult.

LET'S PRAY >>>

Saint Paul, help us understand the Bible and listen carefully to the readings at Mass. Amen.

For a multimedia glossary of Catholic Faith Words, Sunday readings, seasonal and Saint resources, and chapter activities go to **aliveinchrist.osv.com**.

Chapter 17 Review

A **Work with Words** Match the description in Column A to the correct word or words in Column B.

Column A   Column B

1. Short stories about everyday life that Jesus told.   teach

2. The first main part of the Mass.   parables

3. Jesus used parables to do this.   homily

4. A short talk by the priest or deacon about the readings at Mass.   Liturgy of the Word

5. A statement of the Church's beliefs.   creed

B **Check Understanding** Circle the correct answer.

6. Jesus was a great _____.

   storyteller   farmer   follower

7. Jesus' stories had lessons about God's _____.

   family   friends   love

8. We say the Prayer of _____ together at Mass.

   contrition   the Faithful   the people

9. Jesus' parables teach you how to _____.

   go to Mass   read   follow God

10. The _____ is like a mustard seed.

   Kingdom of God   land   Bible

 Go to **aliveinchrist.osv.com** for an interactive review.

Remembering Jesus' Sacrifice

♥ Let Us Pray

Leader: God, we offer you our praise and thanks.

"I will offer a sacrifice of praise
and call on the name of the LORD."
Psalm 116:17

All: God, we offer you our praise and thanks. Amen.

📖 God's Word

Jesus said to his followers, "You cannot serve two masters." He told them that God must be first in their lives, not money, not things that they own, or things that they want to get. Based on Matthew 6:24

❓ What Do You Wonder?

- If you follow Jesus, will you be asked to sacrifice?

- What does it mean to say that God is first in your life?

Making Sacrifices

What sacrifice did Jesus make for us?

Giving up something and making a **sacrifice** for someone else can be very difficult. Sacrifice takes love and courage. A rich young man found this out when he asked Jesus about life with God forever.

Catholic Faith Words

sacrifice giving up something out of love for someone else or for the common good (good of everyone). Jesus sacrificed his life for all people.

Last Supper the meal Jesus shared with his disciples on the night before he died. At the Last Supper, Jesus gave himself in the Eucharist.

🔹 God's Word

The Rich Young Man

Jesus said to him, "If you wish to be perfect, go, sell what you have and give to [the] poor, and you will have treasure in heaven. Then come, follow me."

When the young man heard this . . . he went away sad, for he had many possessions. Matthew 19:21–22

The rich young man could not make the sacrifice because he loved his things more than he loved God.

DONATE HAIR

Draw one thing you would give up to make a sacrifice.

The Greatest Gift

People sometimes make sacrifices, but Jesus chose to make the greatest sacrifice of all. Jesus' sacrifice is that he freely gave up his life on a Cross to save all people from the power of sin and everlasting death. He made this sacrifice so that you would have new life with God forever.

God the Father rewarded Jesus for his loving choice. Through God's loving power, Jesus overcame death and was raised to new life.

The Mass is a memorial celebration of Jesus' Death, Resurrection, and Ascension. Jesus' great sacrifice is celebrated at every Mass when we follow his command to do what he did when he shared a final meal with his disciples at the **Last Supper**.

Share Your Faith

Think Write about a time when you gave up something for someone else or when someone else gave up something for you.

_____

_____

_____

Share your answer with a partner.

Members of the assembly bring forward the gifts of bread and wine during the Liturgy of the Eucharist.

Liturgy of the Eucharist
What will the gifts of bread and wine become during the Mass?

The second main part of the Mass is called the **Liturgy of the Eucharist**. Those gathered remember in a special way Jesus' Death, Resurrection, and Ascension.

The Liturgy of the Eucharist begins when members of the assembly bring forward the gifts of bread and wine. The people offer these gifts to God as a sign of their love. The priest prepares the gifts. He asks God to bless them. They will become the Body and Blood of Jesus Christ.

Now, another important part of the celebration begins. The priest leads the assembly in prayer.

Priest: "The Lord be with you."

All: "And with your spirit."

Priest: "Lift up your hearts."

All: "We lift them up to the Lord."

Priest: "Let us give thanks to the Lord our God."

All: "It is right and just."

Catholic Faith Words

Liturgy of the Eucharist the second main part of the Mass that includes Holy Communion

consecration through the power of the Holy Spirit and the words and actions of the priest, the gifts of bread and wine become the Body and Blood of Jesus

Underline the gifts brought forward during the Liturgy of the Eucharist.

© Our Sunday Visitor

246 Chapter 18

The Eucharistic Prayer

The priest now begins the Eucharistic Prayer. He gives praise and thanks to God. He asks the Father to send the Holy Spirit. The priest repeats what Jesus said at the Last Supper:

Priest: FOR THIS IS MY BODY,
WHICH WILL BE GIVEN UP FOR YOU . . .

FOR THIS IS THE CHALICE OF MY BLOOD, . . .
WHICH WILL BE POURED OUT FOR YOU AND
FOR MANY FOR THE FORGIVENESS OF SINS.
DO THIS IN MEMORY OF ME.

This is called the **consecration**. The bread and wine are now the Body and Blood of Christ. The assembly prays the Mystery of Faith:

All: We proclaim your Death, O Lord, and profess your Resurrection until you come again.

The assembly recalls all that Jesus did and offers the Father the gift of his Son. The prayer ends with everyone saying or singing the "Great Amen."

Connect Your Faith

Find the Word Color each X with one color and each O with a different color to find the word you say at the end of the Eucharistic Prayer.

Remembering Jesus' Sacrifice **247**

Our Catholic Life

How do you remember Jesus' sacrifice at Mass?

At Mass, the priest prays the Eucharistic Prayer. After he consecrates the bread and wine he invites everyone to say aloud what we believe about Jesus' sacrifice. He says the words *Mystery of Faith* to the assembly. We answer the priest by praying or singing a Mystery of Faith.

The Mystery of Faith is not a puzzle or a riddle. It is God's love for us, which is greater than we can ever understand completely. So, we simply say what we believe and thank God in our hearts.

Place a check mark next to one you've sung during Mass.

The Mystery of Faith

1. We proclaim your Death, O Lord, and profess your Resurrection until you come again.

2. When we eat this Bread and drink this Cup, we proclaim your Death, O Lord, until you come again.

3. Save us, Savior of the world, for by your Cross and Resurrection, you have set us free.

People of Faith

Blessed Imelda Lambertini, 1322–1333

Blessed Imelda Lambertini lived at a time when children couldn't receive Holy Communion until they were twelve. She was too young to receive Communion but she would pray at Mass and make a "spiritual communion." Jesus would come into her heart, but she still wanted to receive the Body of Christ in the Eucharist. One day, she was praying at Mass and a beautiful light with a host in it appeared over her head. Blessed Imelda is the patron Saint of children receiving their First Communion.

May 13

Discuss: What is one message about Jesus you can share with someone?

 Learn more about Blessed Imelda at **aliveinchrist.osv.com**

Live Your Faith

Design A Window Choose one of the three Mysteries of Faith and design your own stained glass window using symbols and pictures that remind people of this statement of faith.

Remembering Jesus' Sacrifice **249**

Let Us Pray

Prayer of Remembrance

Gather and begin with the Sign of the Cross.

Leader: God our Father, your Son Jesus gave his life for us. Be with us as we pray.

Reader: A reading from the First Letter of Paul to the Corinthians.

Read 1 Corinthians 11:23–26.

The Word of the Lord.

All: Thanks be to God.

 Sing "We Proclaim Your Death, O Lord"

We proclaim your Death, O Lord.
    Jesus died for us.
We profess your Resurrection.
    Jesus lives with us.
Until you come again,
we wait in joyful hope!

© 2011, John Burland. All rights reserved.

FAMILY+FAITH
LIVING AND LEARNING TOGETHER

YOUR CHILD LEARNED >>>

This chapter discusses how we celebrate Jesus' sacrifice and gift of himself in the Eucharist at Mass.

God's Word

Read **Matthew 6:24** to see what Jesus says about sacrifice and serving God.

Catholics Believe

- The Eucharist is a memorial of the sacrifice Jesus made.
- The Liturgy of the Eucharist is the second main part of the Mass.

To learn more, go to the *Catechism of the Catholic Church* #1356–1358 at **usccb.org**.

People of Faith

This week, your child met Blessed Imelda Lambertini, the patron Saint of children receiving First Communion.

CHILDREN AT THIS AGE >>>

How They Understand the Liturgy of the Eucharist Many second-grade children have heard the words of the Liturgy of the Eucharist without fully realizing or understanding what they mean. It is hard for children this age to understand how and why Jesus gave himself as a sacrifice for all of humanity. The ritual form of this portion of the Mass will help your child to continue to reflect upon and grow in his or her understanding of Christ's sacrifice and its meaning for each of us.

CONSIDER THIS >>>

What have you sacrificed for your children as a gift of love?

Becoming a parent sets one on a lifelong journey of sacrifice—sacrifices that come from love. This love gives us a glimpse of the love and sacrifice of Jesus. "In a self-centered culture where people are taught to extend themselves only for something in return, the sacrifices each of us make, following the example of Jesus, who freely sacrificed his life in love for all, point to the reality and power of God's love for us" (*USCCA, p. 221*).

LET'S TALK >>>

- Have your child explain what a sacrifice is and how Jesus sacrificed for us.
- Talk with your child about when he or she will have First Communion.

LET'S PRAY >>>

Blessed Imelda Lambertini, pray to God for us that we may receive Holy Communion with reverence. Amen.

For a multimedia glossary of Catholic Faith Words, Sunday readings, seasonal and Saint resources, and chapter activities go to **aliveinchrist.osv.com**.

Chapter 18 Review

A **Work with Words** Write the letter of the correct word or words from the Word Bank to complete each sentence.

1. Jesus' great [b] was his Death on the Cross.

2. The [e] become the Body and Blood of Jesus.

3. Jesus said, "Do this in [a] of me."

4. At the end of the Eucharistic Prayer, the people say, [c].

5. The [d] is a memorial of Jesus' Death, Resurrection, and Ascension.

B **Check Understanding** Draw a line to complete the sentences in Column A with the correct words in Column B.

Column A	Column B
6. At Mass, the priest prays the	Eucharistic Prayer.
7. We remember what Jesus said at	God's love for us.
8. The second main part of the Mass is the	the Last Supper.
9. The Mystery of Faith is	Liturgy of the Eucharist.
10. The Eucharistic Prayer ends with the	Great Amen.

Go to **aliveinchrist.osv.com** for an interactive review.

252 Chapter 18 Review

© Our Sunday Visitor

A **Work with Words** Complete each sentence with the correct word from the Word Bank.

Word Bank

Eucharist

Word

assembly

Mass

creed

1. _Mass_ is another name for the celebration of the Sacrament of the Eucharist.

2. In the Liturgy of the _Word_, stories from the Bible are read.

3. The people gathered together at Mass make up the _assembly_.

4. The Liturgy of the _eucharist_ is the second main part of the Mass.

5. A _creed_ is a statement of the Church's beliefs.

B **Check Understanding** Draw a line from the description in Column A to the correct word or words in Column B.

Column A	Column B
6. This is said at the end of the Eucharistic Prayer.	Jesus' Sacrifice
7. The bread and wine become this.	Homily
8. A short talk by the priest or deacon about Scripture readings.	"Great Amen"
9. The priest or deacon reads this.	Christ's Body and Blood
10. The Mass celebrates this.	The Gospel

Write T if the sentence is TRUE. Write F if the sentence is FALSE.

11. ☐ The priest leads the assembly in celebrating the Mass.

12. ☐ At Mass you do not take part in the celebration.

13. ☐ Jesus' stories are called parables.

14. ☐ Jesus' parables teach us about God's love.

15. ☐ The Mass is a memorial celebration of Peter's birth, life, and death.

C **Make Connections** Circle the correct answer.

16. As Mass begins, the assembly _____.

    sits   kneels   stands and sings

17. A _____ is giving up something out of love.

    sacrifice   celebration   trade

18. At the _____ Jesus shared a meal with his disciples.

    Resurrection   Last Supper   Ascension

19. Jesus' stories always had lessons about _____.

    history   animals   God's love

20. The Mass celebrates Jesus' Death and _____.

    family   Resurrection   Father

Write about parts of the Mass that remind you of each of the parts of a family meal described below.

21. Your cousins come for Sunday dinner.

_____

_____

22. Your family welcomes everyone once they are together.

_____

_____

23. Family members tell stories during the meal.

_____

_____

24. Family members bring food and drink to share.

_____

_____

25. Your family shares a meal of food and drink.

_____

_____

_____

Kingdom of God

Our Catholic Tradition

- The Eucharist unites us with Jesus and with one another. We share the same mission to love the way Jesus did. (CCC, 1396)

- Jesus, the Lamb, is really and truly present in Holy Communion. We call this Real Presence. (CCC, 1380)

- The Eucharist is a sign of what Heaven will be like—happiness forever with God. We spread the news of the Kingdom to everyone. (CCC, 562, 1419)

How does receiving Holy Communion help us on our journey to Heaven?

Christ the Redeemer Statue, Rio de Janerio, Brazil

Supper of the Lamb

♥ Let Us Pray

CHAPTER 19

Leader: We praise you God, for you are good and holy.

The earth has yielded its harvest;
God, our God, blesses us.   Psalm 67:7

All: O God, we thank you for sharing your harvest
with us in Holy Communion. Amen.

📖 God's Word

Once, the people wanted a sign from Jesus so that they could better see and believe in him. They said, "Our ancestors ate manna in the desert, as it is written: 'He gave them bread from heaven to eat.'" Jesus said to them, "Amen, amen, I say to you, it was not Moses who gave the bread from heaven; my Father gives you the true bread from heaven. For the bread of God is that which comes down from heaven and gives life to the world. I say to you, I am the bread of life; whoever comes to me will never hunger, and whoever believes in me will never thirst."

Based on John 6:30–35

❓ What Do You Wonder?

- How does Jesus feed us today?
- How does the Father take care of us?

Jesus Feeds Us

How does Jesus provide for us?

Jesus knew how important food was for life. The Gospels have many stories of Jesus sharing meals with his friends.

Catholic Faith Words

Holy Communion receiving Jesus' Body and Blood in the celebration of the Eucharist

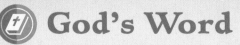

God's Word

The Feeding of Five Thousand

One day, Jesus was speaking to a crowd of five thousand people. Late in the day, the Apostles told Jesus to send the crowds away to nearby villages to find food.

Jesus told the Apostles to feed the people themselves. "How can we do that?" they asked. "We have only five loaves of bread and two fish."

Jesus told them to have the people sit down. He took the bread and fish, looked up to Heaven, and blessed the food. He broke it into pieces and gave the pieces to his followers to pass out among the people.

Everyone had enough to eat. The leftovers filled twelve straw baskets. Based on Luke 9:10–17

The Lord's Prayer

When Jesus fed the people, they felt his love and care. Jesus continues to care for us. In the Mass, he gives us his Body and Blood. The Mass is the Supper of the Lamb. Jesus is the Lamb of God because of his sacrifice for us. He invites us to his supper where he feeds us in the Eucharist.

As we prepare to receive **Holy Communion**, we stand to say the Lord's Prayer. We praise the Father and ask that he reign in our hearts and lives. We show our trust in him for all we need now and to be with him forever.

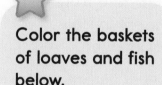

Color the baskets of loaves and fish below.

Share Your Faith

Think What did Jesus feed the crowd in the story? How does Jesus feed us in the Mass?

Share Break into two groups and talk about it.

Supper of the Lamb **259**

Holy Communion
What happens after the Lord's Prayer?

After praying to our Father, we offer the peace of Christ to one another. This sign of peace is a reminder that we share with others the peace, love, and goodwill that comes from Christ and unites us.

After the sign of peace, the priest breaks the Host that is the Body of Christ before he eats and shares it. This is what Jesus did at the Last Supper. The priest's action again reminds the assembly that Jesus died and was raised from the dead for all people. If you are free from serious sin, you are welcome at the Lord's table. Jesus is really and truly present in Holy Communion. We call this **Real Presence**. When you receive Holy Communion, you become one with Jesus and all his Church.

Catholic Faith Words

Real Presence the teaching that Jesus is really and truly with us in the Eucharist. We receive Jesus in his fullness.

Underline who is really and truly present in Holy Communion.

We offer the sign of peace during Mass by shaking hands or hugging one another.

© Our Sunday Visitor

Receiving Communion

The Body and Blood of Jesus is a great gift. When you receive it, you show **reverence**, or care and respect. You walk to the altar prayerfully. As the person in front of you receives the Eucharist, you bow slightly. When it is your turn, the priest, deacon, or an extraordinary minister of Holy Communion says, "The Body of Christ," and you say, "Amen." You receive the Body of Christ in your hand or on your tongue. You may also receive the Blood of Christ from the chalice.

Afterwards, you go back to your place and sing with everyone. Then you pray in silence.

The Blessed Sacrament

Any Hosts reserved, or left over, after Mass are stored in a beautiful cabinet or container called the **Tabernacle**. Jesus remains present in the reserved Hosts, which are also called the **Blessed Sacrament**.

Catholic Faith Words

reverence the care and respect you show to God and holy persons and things

Blessed Sacrament a name for the Holy Eucharist, especially the Body of Christ kept in the Tabernacle

Tabernacle the special place in the church where the Blessed Sacrament is reserved after Mass for those who are ill or for Eucharistic Adoration

Connect Your Faith

Show Reverence Write one good action that you can do to show reverence during Mass.

_____

_____

_____

Our Catholic Life

How do we honor Jesus in the Eucharist outside of Mass?

Some people cannot join the community at Mass. They may be sick at home or in the hospital. Some elderly people are too weak to travel. All these people are still a part of the assembly. They are still joined to the community in prayer. After Mass, they may be visited by the priest, a deacon, or an extraordinary minister of Holy Communion who brings Holy Communion to them and prays with them.

Any other Hosts reserved after Mass are placed in the Tabernacle. A lamp or candle always burns near the Tabernacle to remind people that Jesus is present.

Draw a box around the word "Tabernacle." What is kept inside the Tabernacle?

Outside of Mass, people can spend time in prayer before the Blessed Sacrament kept in the Tabernacle.

© Our Sunday Visitor

People of Faith

Venerable Pierre Toussaint, 1766–1853

Venerable Pierre Toussaint was a slave born in Haiti. His owner taught him to read and write. When his owner's family moved to New York City, they brought Pierre with them. Pierre became a barber and helped support his owner's family after the man died. He and his wife raised his niece and Pierre often took her for walks in the city. He was well known for his generosity and aid to the poor. He attended daily Mass and had a great love for Jesus in Holy Communion. He helped build St. Patrick's Old Cathedral in New York.

Discuss: How can you show respect for Jesus in the Eucharist?

Learn more about Venerable Pierre Toussaint at **aliveinchrist.osv.com**

Live Your Faith

Make a Prayer Card Decorate the front of the prayer card and write a prayer for parish members who cannot be present at Mass.

Let Us Pray

Prayer of Petition

Gather and begin with the Sign of the Cross.

Leader: Let's pray the words of Saint Padre Pio, to ask Christ to be with us always.

Reader 1: Stay with me, Lord, for it is necessary to have you present so that I do not forget you. You know how easily I abandon you.

Stay with me, Lord, because I am weak and I need your strength, that I may not fall so often.

Stay with me, Lord, for you are my life…

Reader 2: Stay with me, Lord, for you are my light and without you I am in darkness.

Stay with me, Lord, to show me your will.

Stay with me, Lord, so that I hear your voice and follow you.

All: Stay with me, Lord, for I desire to love you very much and always be in your company…Amen.

Saint Padre Pio, Prayer After Communion

Sing "The Supper of the Lamb"

The Supper of the Lamb
The Body of our Lord
The Blood of Christ outpoured
The Supper of the Lamb
The gift of life anew
A gift of love for you
For you are called to the
Supper of the Lamb

© 2011, John Burland. All rights reserved.

Tabernacle

FAMILY+FAITH
LIVING AND LEARNING TOGETHER

YOUR CHILD LEARNED >>>

This chapter explains how we are united with Jesus and with one another when we reverently receive Holy Communion.

God's Word

Read **Matthew 14:15–21** to learn about the multiplication of the loaves and fishes.

Catholics Believe

- Through the Eucharist, Jesus' followers are united with him and one another.
- The gift of Holy Communion is received with reverence.

To learn more, go to the *Catechism of the Catholic Church* #319, 256, 454 at **usccb.org**.

People of Faith

This week, your child met Venerable Pierre Toussaint, a former slave who was well known for his love of the Eucharist and care for the poor.

CHILDREN AT THIS AGE >>>

How They Understand the Real Presence of Jesus Christ in the Eucharist Transubstantiation, the transformation of the bread and wine during Mass to the Body and Blood of Jesus Christ, seems like a very difficult concept to impart to children. However, many children's stories and movies have examples of things or people that have taken the form of something else (shape shifters, etc.). Therefore, they are capable of understanding that the Eucharist still looks and tastes like bread and wine but is Jesus himself.

CONSIDER THIS >>>

Have you ever wondered why we call Jesus' Body and Blood, "Communion"?

Communion is another name for Eucharist because the word describes an effect of Eucharist. When we receive the gift of Jesus' Body and Blood, we enter into communion with him. In Christ we are then made one with each other. "We testify in faith that God as Trinity wants to relate to us and to be engaged in our world…love within the Trinity makes possible a divine closeness to us. Love preserves the mystery and yet overcomes what might have been a gulf between us and God. Unity and communion with God in the Church also calls us to become a source of unity for all people" (*USCCA, p. 119*).

LET'S TALK >>>

- Have your child show you the way to receive Holy Communion. Ask children what they do (bow, hold out cupped hands, etc.) and what they say (Amen).
- Talk about why your family would stay after Mass to say a prayer in front of the Tabernacle.

LET'S PRAY >>>

Venerable Pierre, pray for us that we may help others see the presence of Jesus in the Eucharist. Amen.

For a multimedia glossary of Catholic Faith Words, Sunday readings, seasonal and Saint resources, and chapter activities go to **aliveinchrist.osv.com**.

Chapter 19 Review

 A **Work with Words** Use the word or words from the Word Bank to complete the sentences.

1. Real _____Presence_____ is Jesus really and truly with us in the Eucharist.

2. ____Holy Communion____ is receiving the Body and Blood of Christ.

3. All Hosts reserved after Mass are placed in the ____Tabernacle____.

4. ____Reverence____ is the care and respect you show to God and holy persons and things.

5. The ____Blessed Sacrament____ is the name we give to the Body of Christ reserved in the Tabernacle.

B **Check Understanding** Use the numbers 1 to 5 to put the sentences in the order they happen at Mass.

6. [ ] The priest breaks the bread.

7. [ ] All stand to pray the Lord's Prayer.

8. [ ] After Communion the people continue to sing and then pray in silence.

9. [ ] The people offer the sign of peace.

10. [ ] The people receive Holy Communion.

 Go to **aliveinchrist.osv.com** for an interactive review.

© Our Sunday Visitor

Go Forth!

♥ Let Us Pray

Leader: God, as we go forth, be with us.

May God be merciful to us and bless us…
so that the whole world may know your will.
Based on Psalm 67:2–3

All: Thank you, God, for going with us as we share you with others. Amen.

📖 God's Word

"[Paul] remained for two full years in his lodgings. He received all who came to him, and with complete assurance…he proclaimed the kingdom of God and taught about the Lord Jesus Christ." **Acts 28:30–31**

? What Do You Wonder?

- Why is the mission of Jesus important to us today?

- How do you tell others about Jesus' mission?

267

Live the Gospel

How do we share the Good News?

After receiving Holy Communion, we may hear some announcements. Then, the priest or deacon blesses us and says the Mass has ended. He dismisses us to, "Go in peace." We respond, "Thanks be to God." This final part of the Mass is called the Concluding Rites.

We are sent to proclaim the Good News and give honor to God by the way we live. Jesus' first followers took his Good News to people everywhere.

Catholic Faith Words

mission a job or purpose. The Church's mission is to announce the Good News of God's Kingdom.

missionaries people who answer God's call to bring the message of Jesus and announce the Good News of his Kingdom to people in other places

God's Word

Peter Preaches

Peter told the people of Jerusalem that Jesus sent the Apostles to preach to all people.

The Apostles shared the Good News of God's Kingdom. Peter told the people that Jesus wanted everyone to believe in him. If they believed, they would receive forgiveness through Jesus' name.

After listening to Peter, many people from faraway places asked to be baptized. Peter told the crowd that anyone who was moved by the Spirit could be baptized. Based on Acts 10:42–48

The Church's Mission

Peter and the other Apostles shared Jesus' Good News and led the Church. The Pope and bishops follow the Apostles in this role. They lead the Church in her work to spread the Good News of Jesus and God's Kingdom throughout the world. This work is called the Church's **mission**. All her members share this responsibility.

Most Church members share Jesus' message right where they are. Others bring the message of Jesus to faraway places. They are called **missionaries**.

Missionaries travel to countries around the world and help people meet their basic needs.

Share Your Faith

Think What can you do to bring Jesus' message of love to others?

_____

_____

_____

_____

Share With a partner, talk about your responses.

An Example for All
What did Mother Cabrini do?

Everyone has different gifts. We can use those talents to spread Jesus' message in different ways.

Saint Frances Xavier Cabrini

Frances Xavier Cabrini was born in a small village in Italy. She was sickly throughout her life, but this did not stop her from doing God's work.

After hearing stories about the Saints, Frances wanted to be a missionary in China. She wanted to be a religious sister, but was thought too sickly to join any group. So she started her own community. Pope Leo XIII suggested Frances go to the United States to help Italian immigrants that had just arrived.

© Our Sunday Visitor

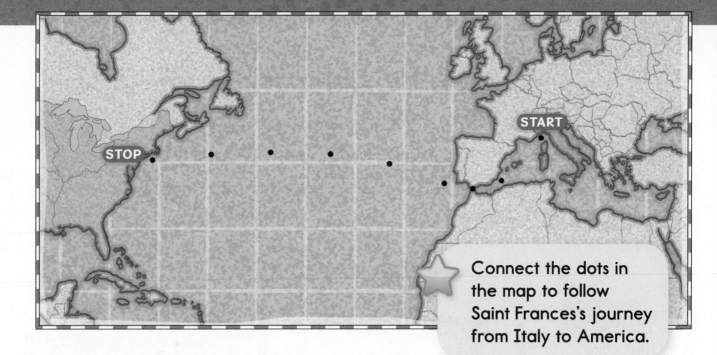

Connect the dots in the map to follow Saint Frances's journey from Italy to America.

Although she had a great fear of water, she crossed the ocean to New York. There she set up a home for orphaned Italian girls and other services for those who were poor.

By the time she was sixty-seven years old, Frances had set up over sixty schools, hospitals, orphanages, and convents throughout the world. In 1917 she died. In 1946, Frances became the first United States citizen to be named a Saint of the Catholic Church. She had carried out the Church's mission, bringing the love of Jesus to those in need.

Connect Your Faith

Spread the Good News If you could go anywhere in the world to tell others about Jesus' love, where would you go?

_____

_____

Our Catholic Life

Who can help you learn about Jesus?

Learning about Jesus is a journey that lasts your whole life. There is always more to learn. It's a good thing there are many people who can help you. They are your guides on the journey, helping you grow in faith.

Priest
- Celebrates Mass and the Sacraments
- Gives homilies to help us understand the Bible

Deacon
- Proclaims the Gospel at Mass
- Serves and helps those who are sick or in need

Extraordinary Minister of Holy Communion
- Helps give Holy Communion at Mass
- Brings Holy Communion to people who cannot attend Mass

Director of Religious Education
- Plans programs for everyone who wants to learn more about Jesus

Catechist or Religion Teacher
- Teaches children and adults about Jesus
- Prepares children to receive the Sacraments

How can you teach others about God's love this week?

You

_____

_____

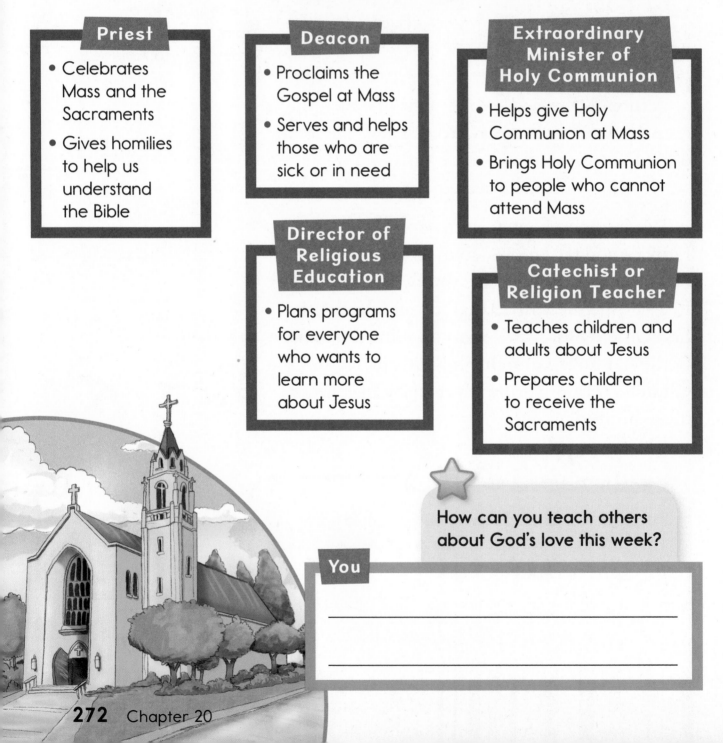

People of Faith

Saint Anthony Claret, 1807–1870

October 24

Saint Anthony Mary Claret was born in Spain. His father taught him to weave and make designs. He also learned how to print books. Later, he became a priest and then a bishop. Saint Anthony used his skills to spread the message of Jesus. He went to Cuba as a missionary. He also started a company that printed religious books. He wrote more than 100 books himself. He started an order of priests called the Claretians. They continue his work today.

Discuss: What skills can you use to help others learn about Jesus?

 Learn more about Saint Anthony at **aliveinchrist.osv.com**

Live Your Faith

Tell Describe what is happening in the picture.

Show Draw a picture of yourself teaching someone else about Jesus.

♡ **Let Us Pray**

Blessing Prayer

Gather and begin with the Sign of the Cross.

Leader: Make a Sign of the Cross on your forehead.
May you always remember to follow Jesus.

All: Amen.

Leader: Make a Sign of the Cross over your closed eyes.
May you learn to see Jesus in all whom you meet.

All: Amen.

Leader: Make a Sign of the Cross on your lips.
May all your words show respect.

All: Amen.

Leader: Make a Sign of the Cross over your heart.
May love move you to action and may God
give you strength to carry on the work of Jesus.

All: Amen.

 Sing "Share the Light"

Share the light of Jesus.
Share the light that shows the way.
Share the light of Jesus.
Share God's spirit today.
Share God's spirit today.

Repeat Verse

Share the word…
Share the love…
Share the smile…
Share the light…

FAMILY+FAITH
LIVING AND LEARNING TOGETHER

YOUR CHILD LEARNED >>>

This chapter explains how we are sent from the Mass to live out the Church's mission of sharing Jesus' message of love and the Kingdom of God.

God's Word

Read **Acts 28:30–31** to learn more about Saint Paul and his mission.

Catholics Believe

- The Church's mission is to share Jesus' love and to announce the Good News of the Kingdom of God.
- All members of the Church share in her mission.

To learn more, go to the *Catechism of the Catholic Church* #900–905 at **usccb.org**.

People of Faith

This week, your child met Saint Anthony Mary Claret, the founder of the Claretians. He used his skills as a printer to produce books about the Catholic faith.

CHILDREN AT THIS AGE >>>

How They Understand Living as a Eucharistic People
Children have sometimes been told "you are what you eat" as a way of helping them understand that they should eat healthy things that will help them grow and stay away from too much junk food. They should be prepared for the idea that as they nourish themselves with Jesus himself in the form of the Eucharist, God will help them to become more like Christ in their daily lives. In fact, we are sent forth after the Eucharistic celebration to be the hands and feet of Christ in the world.

CONSIDER THIS >>>

How hard is it to keep good news to yourself?

We use the phrase, "bursting with good news" because it describes how difficult it is to keep good news to ourselves. The Good News that changed all of humanity was the life, Death, and Resurrection of Jesus. And we should be simply bursting with that Good News. "It is the Good News that results in love, justice, and mercy for the whole world. The Kingdom is realized partially on earth and permanently in heaven. We enter this Kingdom through faith in Christ, baptismal initiation into the Church, and life in communion with all her members" (*USCCA, p. 79-80*).

LET'S TALK >>>

- Have your child explain the Church's mission (spreading the Good News and working for the Kingdom).
- Share how God nourishes you through the Sacraments, your family, prayer, art, and so on.

LET'S PRAY >>>

Saint Anthony, pray for us that we may use our skills to teach others about Jesus. Amen.

For a multimedia glossary of Catholic Faith Words, Sunday readings, seasonal and Saint resources, and chapter activities go to **aliveinchrist.osv.com**.

Chapter 20 Review

A **Work with Words** Write the letter of the correct words from the Word Bank to complete each sentence.

1. Saint [b] was a missionary who worked in the United States.

2. Jesus' message of God's saving love is called the [e].

3. The Church's [a] is to spread the Good News.

4. A [c] is a person sent to bring the Good News of Jesus to people in faraway places.

5. All the members of the [d] share in her mission.

B **Check Understanding** Draw a line from the roles in Column A to the correct descriptions in Column B.

Column A	Column B
6. Director of Religious Education	serves and proclaims the Gospel at Mass
7. Catechist	celebrates Mass and the Sacraments
8. Extraordinary Minister	teaches about Jesus
9. Deacon	plans programs to help others learn about Jesus
10. Priest	distributes Holy Communion

Go to **aliveinchrist.osv.com** for an interactive review.

A Feast for Everyone

 Let Us Pray

Leader: Dear God, we know you will be with us always.

Indeed, goodness and mercy will be with me all the days of my life. Based on Psalm 23:6

All: Thank you, God, for guiding and directing us all our life. Amen.

God's Word

"Behold, I stand at the door and knock. If anyone hears my voice and opens the door, [then] I will enter his house and dine with him, and he with me."
Revelation 3:20

? What Do You Wonder?

- How is Jesus with us in our home?
- How can I hear Jesus knocking?

277

All Are Invited

What does God want for each of us?

God the Father invites everyone to the happiness of his great love on this Earth and in **Heaven** forever. Jesus told this story to help people understand that God the Father wants everyone to enjoy this happiness.

Catholic Faith Words

Heaven the full joy of living with God forever

God's Word

The Wedding Feast

Storyteller: A king gave a wedding feast for his son. When everything was ready, the king sent his servants out to invite the guests.

Servants: The feast is ready. It's time to come and celebrate.

Three people: We can't come. We have a lot of work to do. We are very busy.

Storyteller: The servant brought this message home to the king.

King: Go out to the highways and byways. Search all the paths and alleys. Tell everyone to come. I want my house bursting with people.

Storyteller: The servants did just as the king commanded. They invited everybody to come to the banquet. And many people came. Young and old people came. People who were blind came. People who were strong helped people with crutches. Soon the house was full. Based on Matthew 22:2–10 and Luke 14:16–23

Share Your Faith

Think 1. Who did the king invite to the party?

_____

2. Who does the king in this story remind you of?

_____

Share your answers with a partner.

With God Now and Always

How can you accept God's invitation?

God invites you to share in the great feast in Heaven. In Heaven, you will see God face to face.

Until you see him face to face, God gives you the great gift of the Eucharist. The Eucharist is a sign of joy and of what Heaven will be like. Receiving the Eucharist helps you look forward to the day when you will be with God in Heaven.

Every time you receive Holy Communion at Mass, you receive the food that helps you live forever in Jesus Christ.

Say "Yes" to God!

God calls you to know, love, and serve him. You are like the guests in the Bible story. God invites you to share in a great feast. You could refuse to come. Or you can joyfully accept.

> Underline what the Eucharist is a sign of.

God invites you to say "yes" each day. Here are some ways you say "yes" to God.

- Obey the Commandments.

- Listen to God's Word in the Bible.

- Take part in Mass and receive Holy Communion.

- Seek God's forgiveness in the Sacrament of Penance and Reconciliation.

- Forgive and love other people.

- Help people in need.

- Pray to God each day.

Connect Your Faith

Answering God's Call
Draw a picture of a person you know who says "yes" to God.

Our Catholic Life

How did Mary show love for God?

God calls each person to share his love. Mary gladly said "yes" when God asked her to be Jesus' Mother, even though she knew it would not be easy. You can learn from Mary how to show love for God in your own life.

We honor Mary for saying "yes" to God with all her heart, soul, and mind. Praying the Hail Mary is a way to honor Mary.

The Hail Mary

Words of the Prayer	What They Mean
Hail, Mary, full of grace,	Mary, you are filled with God's own life, help, and love.
the Lord is with thee.	You are very close to God.
Blessed art thou among women	God chose you for a very important mission.
and blessed is the fruit of thy womb, Jesus.	The baby that grew inside you is holy and very special.
Holy Mary, Mother of God,	Your child is the Son of God!
pray for us sinners,	Please pray for us, because we don't always say "yes" to God.
now and at the hour of our death.	Be with us now and all through our lives.
Amen.	Yes, we believe this!

People of Faith

Saint Mary Magdalene de Pazzi, 1566—1607

Saint Mary Magdalene de Pazzi was a nun from Italy who spent her whole life in prayer. She thought about Heaven a lot, even when she was sewing. Once, when her friend died, she saw her going into Heaven. Saint Mary Magdalene said that her friend looked like a white bird flying into a beautiful big house. She said that Heaven is beautiful, more beautiful than anything any of us have ever seen.

May 25

Discuss: What do you think Heaven looks like?

 Learn more about Saint Mary Magdalene at **aliveinchrist.osv.com**

Live Your Faith

Write a Story about a time you or someone you know said "yes" to God.

_____

_____

_____

_____

_____

_____

_____

♥ Let Us Pray

Pray with God's Word

Gather and begin with the Sign of the Cross.

Leader: We rejoice that God invites us to Heaven.
He sent Jesus to show us the way.

Reader 1: A reading from the holy Gospel according to John.

Read John 3:16.

The Gospel of the Lord.

All: Praise to you, Lord Jesus Christ.

Leader: Let us pray.

Bow your heads as the leader prays.

All: Amen.

Leader: Go forth and share God's love with one another.

All: Thanks be to God.

 Sing "All That God Wants You to Be"
You can become all that God wants you to be!
Here am I, O Lord! I come to do your will.
Help me become all that you want me to be!

© 2006, Carey Landry. Published by OCP. All rights reserved.

FAMILY+FAITH
LIVING AND LEARNING TOGETHER

YOUR CHILD LEARNED >>>

This chapter explains that the Eucharist is a taste of the great feast of love and happiness we will have with God in Heaven.

God's Word

 Read **Revelation 3:20** to find out how Jesus seeks us and responds when we accept his invitation.

Catholics Believe

- Heaven is the full joy of living with God forever.
- The Eucharist is a sign of joy and of what Heaven will be like.

To learn more, go to the *Catechism of the Catholic Church* #1023–1030 at **usccb.org**.

People of Faith

This week, your child met Saint Mary Magdalene de Pazzi. She said that Heaven is more beautiful than anything ever seen.

CHILDREN AT THIS AGE >>>

How They Understand Eternal Life in Heaven Second-graders often have some limited experience with death. Perhaps a pet or a distant relative has died. This is often difficult for them, but they are comforted by the idea that their loved one is with God in Heaven. Their idea of Heaven may be influenced by what they have seen in cartoons or other media. For example, they might think people in Heaven live on clouds, have wings, and play harps. It is helpful for them to hear that we are not sure what Heaven looks like, but God promises that everyone there is happy—that it is a place of peace and love.

CONSIDER THIS >>>

Have you ever wondered why God created you?

You might even wonder if God has a plan for your life. "We come to know God's plan for us not only through an understanding of our human nature and his created order but also because he speaks directly to us." We must make time to pay attention to God's direction (*USCCA, p. 328*).

LET'S TALK >>>

- Ask your child to share one thing they learned about Heaven.
- Talk about loved ones who have died and how your family remembers and celebrates them.

LET'S PRAY >>>

 Dear God, help us to think about Heaven, like Saint Mary Magdalene, and to want to be with you there forever. Amen.

For a multimedia glossary of Catholic Faith Words, Sunday readings, seasonal and Saint resources, and chapter activities go to **aliveinchrist.osv.com**.

Chapter 21 Review

A **Work with Words** Fill in the blank with the correct word from the Word Bank.

1. God wants people to be _____.

2. God calls us to _____.

3. The _____ is a sign of the joy of Heaven.

4. The Kingdom of Heaven is like a _____.

B **Check Understanding** Write the letter T if the sentence is TRUE. Write the letter F if the sentence is FALSE.

5. [ ] Heaven is the full joy of living with God forever.

6. [ ] God calls only some people to share his love.

7. [ ] Mary gladly said "yes" to God's call to be the Mother of his Son, Jesus.

8. [ ] You honor Mary when you show love for God in your own life.

9. [ ] The Lord's Prayer is about Mary.

10. [ ] When your mother asks you to clean your room, and you do it, you are saying "yes" to God.

 Go to **aliveinchrist.osv.com** for an interactive review.

A **Work with Words** Complete each sentence with the letter of the correct word from the Word Bank.

1. Jesus is the ☐ of God.

2. ☐ is the care and respect you show to God and holy persons and things.

3. A ☐ is a job or purpose.

4. God calls you to know, love, and ☐.

5. The full joy of living with God forever is ☐.

Word Bank

a. Heaven

b. Lamb

c. serve

d. mission

e. reverence

Circle the correct answer.

6. A person who brings the message of Jesus and announces the Good News to people in other places is a ____.

   missionary   **catechist**   **teacher**

7. The Body of Christ received at Mass is ____.

   wine   **Holy Communion**   **a mission**

8. The first American Saint was ____.

   Frances Cabrini   **Saint Peter**   **Pope Leo XIII**

9. When you receive Holy Communion, you are one with ____.

   missionaries   **priests**   **the Church**

10. Jesus teaches that Heaven is like a great ____.

    feast   **fish**   **book**

B **Check Understanding** Unscramble the words to complete each sentence.

11. Hosts placed in the Tabernacle after Mass are called the Blessed **CRAMENSAT**. _____

12. People at home or in the hospital are still joined to the community in **YAERPR**. _____

13. After Mass, people who are ill may be visited by a priest, a deacon, or an extraordinary minister of Holy Communion who brings the **HUISECTRA**. _____

C **Make Connections** Write the letter T if the sentence is TRUE. Write the letter F if the sentence is FALSE.

14. ☐ Jesus is really and truly present in the Eucharist.

15. ☐ At the end of Mass we are sent out to "Go in peace," and proclaim the Good News.

16. ☐ Jesus sends you on a mission to teach other people about yourself.

17. ☐ Mary always said "yes" to God.

18. ☐ Praying the Lord's Prayer is one way you praise the Father and ask for his help.

19. ☐ We offer each other the Sign of Peace after we receive Holy Communion.

20. ☐ God calls only priests and missionaries to share his love.

Complete each sentence below with the correct answer.

21. Walking to the altar prayerfully is showing

_____.

22. The Holy Communion that you receive at Mass is

_____.

23. Sharing the Good News of Jesus and God's Kingdom throughout the world is the Church's

_____.

24. A catechist or religion teacher helps children by

_____.

25. Praying the Hail Mary is a way to honor

_____.

Live Your Faith
Catholic Social Teaching

Life and Dignity

We read in the Bible that God knew us before we were even born: "Before I formed you...I knew you" (Jeremiah 1:5). God created each one of us. He has a plan for our lives. He knows what he made us to be.

Every life is valuable to God. Because God made each person, we should be kind and fair to everyone. We should take care of the bodies and minds God gave us and use them to do good things.

God wants us to be nice to others, and talk about problems instead of fighting. If we see someone else being mean, we should speak up, and get help if necessary. We should try to protect others because every life is important to God.

Respect Each Person

God created you in his own image. There is no one else exactly like you. God blessed you with many gifts and talents. God did this for everyone!

Sometimes it is easy to forget this good news. You might think of the things you can't do, or the things you don't like about someone else. But God calls you to treat all people, yourself included, with respect. You are wonderfully made!

≫ **How can you show respect for yourself and others?**

Share the Good News

Write the name of someone you want to share the Good News with.

_____

1. Write one reason why you care for him or her.

_____

_____

2. Name some of the gifts and talents that make this person special.

_____

_____

Call to Community

God gives us families and communities because he knows it would not be good for us to live our lives alone. In fact, the Bible says that this is why God created Eve to be a companion and friend to Adam, the first human being. (See Genesis 2:18.)

The Church teaches that God gives us families to help us learn who God is and how to love one another. Our parish community also helps us to learn about God. In families and in parish communities, we work together to take care of one another and to become the people God made us to be.

© Our Sunday Visitor

Get Involved!

God made people to live in families and communities to share God's love. You are part of your own family, and part of the family of all God's People. You are part of many communities— your neighborhood, your school, your parish, and the Church around the world.

The gifts of family and community come with responsibilities, too. God calls everyone to help others so no one is left out, and no one feels alone.

≫ **What are some things that you could do with your family to help in your community?**

LIGHT OF CHRIST

A Catholic emblem of faith for Tiger and Wolf Cub Scouts

Draw a Picture

Draw one way you take part in the life of your family and your community.

Rights and Responsibilities

Because God made every person, everyone has rights and responsibilities. Rights are the freedoms or things every person needs and should have. Responsibilities are our duties, or the things we must do.

Jesus said, "You should love your neighbor as yourself" (Mark 12:31). Following this command means making sure everyone's rights are protected. We also have a responsibility to treat others well and work together for the good of everyone.

Having the Things We Need

Humans need many things to live happy and healthy lives: a safe place to live, clothes, food, clean water, and medical care. These important things are called human rights. All people deserve to have these needs met.

The Church teaches that humans have rights because they are made in God's image. Each person has the responsibility to make sure other people get what they need. We are called to protect the human rights of all people.

≫ **How can we help others get what they need?**

Make a List

List three ways you can be responsible at home and at school. What are some things you can do that will help others?

1. _____

_____

2. _____

_____

3. _____

_____

Option for the Poor

In Scripture, Jesus says that whatever we have done for people who are poor or needy, we have also done for him. (See Matthew 25:40.) We should treat people the same way we would treat Jesus himself. When people need food, drink, clothing, housing, or medical care, or when they are lonely, we should try extra hard to help.

Saint Rose of Lima said, "When we serve the poor and the sick, we serve Jesus." Our Church teaches that we should have special love and care for those who are poor and put their needs first. When we do this, God will bless us.

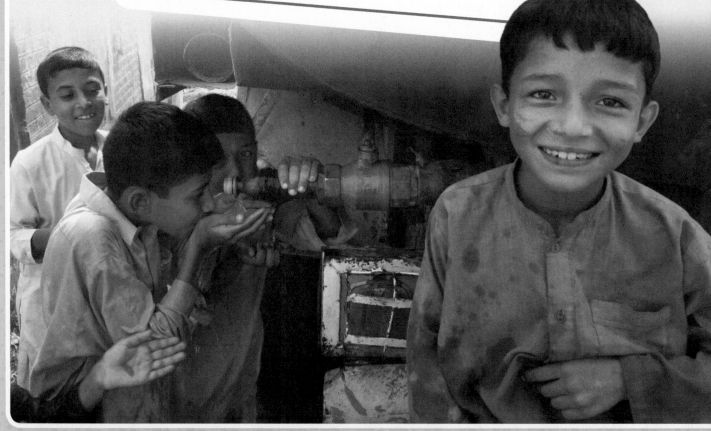

Those Most in Need

One day Jesus was talking with his disciples. They asked him how they could follow him more closely. Jesus told them,

"Whatever you do for your brothers and sisters who are most in need, you do for me. When you care for them, you care for me. When you turn your back on them, you turn your back on me" (Based on Matthew 25:31–46).

Jesus asks us to use the same message. "Look for those who need your care the most," Jesus says. "When you reach out to help them, you will find me."

≫ **Who are the people in your community who are most in need?**

Make a Collage

Glue a picture of Jesus in the space below. Find pictures of people helping others and glue them around Jesus.

Live Your Faith
Catholic Social Teaching

The Dignity of Work

The different jobs people have help them earn money to buy food and other things they need to live. Jobs also allow people to work together with God and his creation. Work is part of God's plan for people, and everyone should work, either in the home or in a job outside the home.

All adults should be able to have a job if they want one. Scripture teaches that workers should be treated fairly by their bosses. (See Deuteronomy 24:14.) They should be given fair pay for their work. (See Leviticus 19:13 and Deuteronomy 24:15.) If workers are unhappy, they should be able to speak up and talk about it with their bosses.

The Value of Work

Work is an important part of life. People work to earn money for both the things they need and want. Many workers take pride in doing their jobs well.

Jesus learned about work from his foster father, Joseph, a carpenter who made beautiful and useful things from wood. And Mary worked hard to teach Jesus and make a loving home.

All kinds of work are important. Workers and bosses have to treat one another with respect. Everyone who works deserves to be paid fairly. No one should work in unsafe conditions.

≫ **Who are some of the workers who help make your life safe, comfortable, and interesting?**

Write a Class Letter

With your catechist's help, write a class letter to the President or to your state senators. Ask your elected leaders to help pass stronger laws that protect the health and safety of workers of all ages.

Live Your Faith
Catholic Social Teaching

Human Solidarity

People around the world are different in many ways. Our hair, eyes, and skin are many different colors. There are people who are rich, people who are poor, and people who are in-between. People believe different things about how we should live.

But one way we are all alike is that God made us. We are one human family. (See Galatians 3:28.) God calls everyone to be his children. Because God made everyone, we should treat everyone with love, kindness, and fairness. In the Beatitudes, Jesus says, "Blessed are the peacemakers" (Matthew 5:9). Treating others fairly will help us to live in peace with one another.

One Human Family

The members of the human family, like the members of your family, may not all look alike. People have different skin colors. They may speak different languages and live in different places. But we are all part of one human family.

Just as you care for your brothers and sisters at home, Jesus wants us to care for our brothers and sisters around the world. One way we can do this is to pray for them.

≫ **How can you care for members of the human family?**

Learn about the Human Family

Choose a country, do some research to find out about the people there, and answer the questions.

1. How are the people are like you?

   _____

2. How are the people different from you?

   _____

3. What could you learn from the people?

   _____

Live Your Faith
Catholic Social Teaching

Care for Creation

God created the whole world—the Earth and sky, the mountains and deserts, and all of the plants, animals, and people. When God made these things, he called them "very good" (Genesis 1:31). God put people in charge of the "fish of the sea, the birds of the air, and all the living things that crawl on the earth" (Genesis 1:28). God wants us to enjoy and take care of everything he has made.

Our Church teaches us that God gave the plants and animals for the good of all people. We need to work to take care of the plants and animals and the places where they live, so everyone can enjoy them now and in the future. We should also be kind to animals, because they are God's creatures.

God's Gifts

God calls you to protect his gifts and to use them wisely. You show God respect when you take care of the planet and all that is in it.

God wants people to have clean water, air, and the food they need to live. The things people do today can help save God's gifts for people to use many years from now.

➤ **What are some ways you can care for God's creation?**

Plan a Garden

Imagine that you are planting a garden. Work with a partner to make your plans.

1. What are two things you would like to grow?

   _____

2. What are some things you need for the garden?

   _____

3. What does the garden need to keep growing?

   _____

4. How would you share your garden?

   _____

Creeds

The Creed tells the faith of the Church. It brings together the Church's most important beliefs about the Holy Trinity and our Catholic faith.

- God the Father, the Creator of all that is.

- Jesus, God's Son and the Savior.

- God the Holy Spirit, helps and guides us as Jesus promised.

- The Church, the Body of Christ in this world.

Apostles' Creed

This creed gives a summary of the Apostles' beliefs. It is often used at Mass during the season of Easter and in Masses with children. This creed is part of the Rosary.

I believe in God,
the Father almighty,
Creator of heaven and earth,
and in Jesus Christ, his only Son, our Lord,

At the words that follow, up to and including the Virgin Mary, all bow.

who was conceived by the
   Holy Spirit,
born of the Virgin Mary,
suffered under Pontius Pilate,
was crucified, died and was buried;
he descended into hell;
on the third day he rose again from
   the dead;

he ascended into heaven,
and is seated at the right hand
   of God the Father almighty;
from there he will come to judge
   the living and the dead.

I believe in the Holy Spirit,
the holy catholic Church,
the communion of saints,
the forgiveness of sins,
the resurrection of the body,
and life everlasting. Amen.

Nicene Creed

This creed which is prayed at Mass was written nearly two thousand years ago by leaders of the Church who met at a city named Nicaea. Christians over the centuries have prayed this creed.

I believe in one God,
the Father almighty,
maker of heaven and earth,
of all things visible and invisible.

I believe in one Lord Jesus Christ,
the Only Begotten Son of God,
born of the Father before all ages.
God from God, Light from Light,
true God from true God,
begotten, not made, consubstantial
    with the Father;
through him all things were made.
For us men and for our salvation
he came down from heaven,

At the words that follow, up to and including and became man, *all bow.*

and by the Holy Spirit was incarnate
    of the Virgin Mary, and
    became man.

For our sake he was crucified under
    Pontius Pilate,
he suffered death and was buried,
and rose again on the third day
in accordance with the Scriptures.
He ascended into heaven
and is seated at the right hand of
    the Father.
He will come again in glory
to judge the living and the dead
and his kingdom will have no end.

I believe in the Holy Spirit, the Lord,
    the giver of life,
who proceeds from the Father and
    the Son,
who with the Father and the Son is
    adored and glorified,
who has spoken through the prophets.

I believe in one, holy, catholic and
    apostolic Church.
I confess one Baptism for the
    forgiveness of sins
and I look forward to the resurrection
    of the dead
and the life of the world to come.
    Amen.

The Church

The Church is the community of the People of God. She has many parts that form one body. Christ is her head, and all Catholics are her members. That is why the Church is called the Body of Christ.

Her Mission

Jesus chose Twelve Apostles to share in his work and ministry in a special way. Before his Ascension, Jesus told his Apostles to take his message everywhere.

Pope Francis

The Twelve Apostles

Peter	Philip	Thaddeus
Andrew	Bartholomew	Thomas
James	Matthew	James
John	Simon	Judas

© Our Sunday Visitor

The Church is led by the Pope and bishops, who continue the Apostles' work to spread the Good News of Jesus and God's Kingdom throughout the world. The Church is also a sign of the glory of Heaven meant for everyone.

Mary and the Saints

Mary is the greatest of the Saints because she said "yes" to being the Mother of God. Other holy people are also recognized as Saints. They are remembered on special feast days in the Church year.

The Seven Sacraments

The Seven Sacraments are special signs and celebrations that Jesus gave his Church. They allow us to share in God's life and work. The Sacraments are divided into three groups.

Sacraments of Initiation	The three Sacraments that celebrate membership into the Catholic Church.	• Baptism • Confirmation • Eucharist
Sacraments of Healing	In these Sacraments, God's forgiveness and healing are given to those suffering physical and spiritual sickness.	• Penance and Reconciliation • Anointing of the Sick
Sacraments at the Service of Communion	These Sacraments celebrate people's commitment to serve God and the community and help build up the People of God.	• Holy Orders • Matrimony (Marriage)

Gestures and Actions

To worship means to adore and honor God, especially in the celebration of the Eucharist (Mass) and in prayer. There are certain actions we do during worship. Here are some of them.

- A bow, a bending at the waist of the upper part of your body, or a reverent nod of your head is a gesture of reverence and worship.

- Folded hands is a traditional prayer posture. It is a sign of prayerfulness, humility, and attentiveness to the presence of God.

- When you kneel, you are in a posture of adoration or repentance. When you stand, you are showing respect.

The Church's Seasons

The Church year is a celebration of events in the lives of Jesus, Mary, and the Saints. Every season of the Church's year has special feasts, colors, and symbols.

Advent

We prepare to celebrate God's coming in time through Jesus, and we await Christ's coming at the end of time.

Feasts: Immaculate Conception, Our Lady of Guadalupe

Color: violet

Symbols: Advent wreath, figure of John the Baptist

Christmas

The Church remembers the birth of Jesus and celebrates the coming in time of the Son of God.

Feasts: Christmas, Nativity of the Lord, Epiphany, Baptism of Jesus

Colors: white or gold

Symbols: manger scenes, star of Bethlehem, Jesse tree

Ordinary Time

The Church celebrates the words and works of Jesus. Ordinary Time occurs twice in the year.

Feasts: Corpus Christi, Transfiguration, Solemnity of Christ the King

Color: green

Symbols: vine and branches, Good Shepherd

Lent

We recall our baptismal promises to change our lives through prayer, fasting, and good works.

Feasts: Ash Wednesday, Palm Sunday

Colors: violet (reddish-purple); red on Palm Sunday

Symbols: ashes, Stations of the Cross, palms

Easter Triduum

The three most holy days of the Church, when we remember Jesus' passing from Death to new life.

Feasts: Holy Thursday, Good Friday, Holy Saturday, Easter

Colors: white or gold and red (Good Friday)

Symbols: feet washing, veneration of cross, lighting the Paschal Candle

Easter

The Church celebrates Jesus' Resurrection and the new life that it brings to all.

Feasts: Ascension, Pentecost

Colors: white or gold, red for Pentecost

Symbols: Alleluia, Easter lilies

Sacrament of Eucharist

The Eucharist is a Sacrament of Initiation. It is the great thanksgiving prayer of Jesus and the Church. It is a Catholic's greatest act of worship and prayer to God. The Eucharist is also a sign of the heavenly feast that all are invited to at the end of time. In the celebration, Jesus is fully present with us.

The celebration of the Eucharist is also called the Mass. It has two main parts. The Liturgy of the Word is the first great part of the Mass. During it, the assembly listens to and responds to God's Word written in the Bible. The second main part is the Liturgy of the Eucharist. During it, the priest leads us in offering thanks and praise to God, and we receive Holy Communion.

The Mass always includes:

- the proclamation of the Word of God.
- thanksgiving to God for all his gifts.
- the consecration of bread and wine.
- receiving Christ's Body and Blood in Holy Communion.

Holy Days of Obligation

Because the Mass is so important, Catholics are required to attend Mass on Sundays (or Saturday evening) and Holy Days of Obligation. The United States celebrates six Holy Days of Obligation.

- Christmas, December 25
- Solemnity of Mary, Mother of God, January 1
- Ascension of the Lord, 40 days after Easter or the Seventh Sunday of Easter
- Assumption of Mary, August 15
- All Saints Day, November 1
- Solemnity of the Immaculate Conception, December 8

The Order of Mass

Introductory Rites

1. Entrance Chant
2. Greeting
3. Rite for the Blessing and Sprinkling of Water
4. Penitential Act
5. Kyrie
6. Gloria
7. Collect

Liturgy of the Word

1. First Reading (usually from the Old Testament)
2. Responsorial Psalm
3. Second Reading (from New Testament letters)
4. Gospel Acclamation (Alleluia)
5. Gospel Dialogue
6. Gospel Reading
7. Homily
8. Profession of Faith (Creed)
9. Prayer of the Faithful

Liturgy of the Eucharist

1. Preparation of the Gifts
2. Invitation to Prayer
3. Prayer over the Offerings
4. Eucharistic Prayer
   - Preface Dialogue
   - Preface
   - Preface Acclamation
   - Consecration
   - Mystery of Faith
   - Concluding Doxology
5. Communion Rite
   - The Lord's Prayer
   - Sign of Peace
   - Lamb of God
   - Invitation to Communion
   - Communion
   - Prayer After Communion

Concluding Rites

1. Greeting
2. Blessing
3. Dismissal

Receiving Holy Communion

When you receive Jesus in Holy Communion, you welcome him by showing reverence. These steps can help you.

- Fold your hands and join in the singing as you wait in line.

- Bow slightly as the person before you is receiving.

- When it is your turn, you can receive the Body of Christ in your hand or on your tongue.

- The person who offers you Communion will say, "The Body of Christ." You say, "Amen." Step aside, and chew and swallow the host.

- You may choose to drink from the cup. When the cup is offered to you, the person will say, "The Blood of Christ." You say, "Amen." Take a small sip.

- Return to your place in church.

- Pray quietly in your own words, thanking Jesus for always being with you.

Because it is so important to have Jesus in your life through Holy Communion, the Church tells you to receive Communion frequently. In fact whenever you go to Mass, you should receive Jesus in Holy Communion, but all Catholics are required to at least once a year.

Special Church Objects

 Altar The table where the Eucharist is celebrated.

 **Lectern (ambo)** A stand for announcing God's Word in the readings at Mass.

 Cruets Small bottles of water or wine.

 Tabernacle A special place in the church where the Blessed Sacrament is reserved after Mass for those who are ill or for Eucharistic Adoration.

 Book of Gospels The special book that contains the Gospel readings used at Mass.

 **Candles** Candles lit during Mass are usually beeswax pillars. They show that Christ, the light of the world, is present.

 Chalice The cup for the Blood of Christ.

 **Ciborium** The special container placed in the Tabernacle that holds the Eucharistic Hosts, the Body of Christ.

 Lectionary A special book used at Mass that contains readings from the Old and New Testament.

 Paten The small plate, usually made of silver or gold, used to hold the Body of Christ.

 **Roman Missal** The special book that contains the prayers of the Mass.

Penance and Reconciliation

Even though we try, we do not always live as God wants us to live. Sometimes we need healing and forgiveness. So Jesus gives us the opportunity to experience God's love, mercy, and forgiveness in the Sacrament of Reconciliation. In this Sacrament, if you are truly sorry, God forgives any sins you have committed. Below are the steps of the Sacrament when it's celebrated with several penitents, the people who confess their sins to the priest. All steps but Step 4 are communal.

Step 1: Introductory Rites

Step 2: Reading from Scripture

Step 3: Examination of conscience, litany of contrition (Sometimes an Act of Contrition, which can be found on pages 170 and 323), the Lord's Prayer

Step 4: Each penitent meets individually with a priest for confession, penance, and absolution by the priest

Prayer of Absolution
God, the Father of mercies,
through the death and resurrection of his Son
has reconciled the world to himself
and sent the Holy Spirit among us
for the forgiveness of sins;
through the ministry of the Church
may God give you pardon and peace,
and I absolve you from your sins
in the name of the Father, and of the Son,
and of the Holy Spirit.

Step 5: Closing

Examination of Conscience

God's gift of conscience helps you choose right from wrong. His gift of grace, God's life within, gives you the strength to do what is right. For more on conscience and to learn more about conscience formation, see page 319.

We prepare for the Sacrament of Penance by thinking about how we have followed the Ten Commandments, Beatitudes, and other Church teachings. Questions like the ones below help us know whether what we've done is good or bad, right or wrong. Remember, mistakes and accidents are not intentional. They are not things done on purpose. They are not sins.

- Did I always use God's name with respect?

- Did I show my love for God and others in some way?

- Did I usually say my daily prayers?

- Did I always obey my mother and father?

- Was I kind to those around me, or was I mean?

- Was I fair in the way that I played and worked with others?

- Did I share my things with others?

- Did I avoid taking what belongs to someone else?

- Did I care for my own things and others' things?

- Did I hurt others by calling them names or telling lies about them?

- Did I go to Mass and take part in the celebration?

Sacramentals

The Church has special signs and symbols to remind us of God. They are called sacramentals. A sacramental can be an object, words, gestures, or actions. They are made sacred through the prayers of the Church.

Words	blessings litanies other prayers	
Actions	Sign of the Cross sign of peace genuflection procession	
Objects	crucifix statues holy water candles	palms rosary images medals

The Rosary

The rosary is a sacramental that reminds us of Mary, the Mother of Jesus, and helps us reflect on the events and mysteries in the lives of Jesus and Mary. We honor her with devotions, like the Rosary, and statues.

God's Laws

God desires you to be in relationship with him. To help you do this and to know what is right, he has given you laws.

The Ten Commandments	What They Mean
1 I am the Lord your God: you shall not have strange gods before me.	Make God the most important thing in your life.
2 You shall not take the name of the Lord your God in vain.	Always use God's name in a reverent way.
3 Remember to keep holy the Lord's Day.	Attend Mass and rest on Sunday.
4 Honor your father and your mother.	Love and obey your parents and guardians.
5 You shall not kill.	Be kind to the people and animals God made; care for yourself and others.
6 You shall not commit adultery.	Be respectful of your body.
7 You shall not steal.	Don't take other people's things.
8 You shall not bear false witness against your neighbor.	Always tell the truth.
9 You shall not covet your neighbor's wife.	Keep your thoughts and words clean; don't be jealous of other people's friendships.
10 You shall not covet your neighbor's goods.	Be happy with the things you have; don't be jealous of what other people have.

The Great Commandment

"You shall love the Lord, your God, with all your heart, with all your being, with all your strength, and with all your mind, and your neighbor as yourself." Luke 10:27

The Law of the Gospel

The Beatitudes

Blessed are the poor in spirit,
for theirs is the kingdom of heaven.
Blessed are they who mourn,
for they will be comforted.
Blessed are the meek,
for they will inherit the land.
Blessed are they who hunger and thirst
    for righteousness,
for they will be satisfied.
Blessed are the merciful,
for they will be shown mercy.
Blessed are the clean of heart,
for they will see God.
Blessed are the peacemakers,
for they will be called children of God.
Blessed are they who are persecuted
    for the sake of righteousness,
for theirs is the kingdom of heaven.
Matthew 5:3–10

Jesus' New Commandment

"This is my commandment: love
one another as I have loved you."
John 15:12

Divine Help

What God commands us to
do, he makes possible by his grace.
(See CCC, 2082.) God's grace is
his life and help within you. It
helps you grow in virtue. Virtues
are good spiritual habits that
strengthen you and enable you
to do what is right and good.

These three virtues of faith,
hope, and charity (love) are gifts
from God that help us know and
love him.

Gifts of the Holy Spirit

- Wisdom helps you see yourself and others as God sees you.

- Understanding helps you get along with others.

- Counsel (right judgment) helps you make good choices.

- Fortitude (courage) helps you act bravely.

- Knowledge helps you know God better.

- Piety (reverence) helps you pray every day.

- Fear of the Lord (wonder and awe) helps you understand how
  great and powerful God is.

Forming Your Conscience

Our conscience is the God-given ability that helps us judge whether our actions are right or wrong. It is important for us to know God's laws so our conscience can help us make good decisions.

It is your job to strengthen, or form, your conscience. This is something you will do throughout your life. We continue to educate our conscience as we grow older. Strengthening your conscience helps your heart be peaceful and loving. It is also necessary for making good choices.

But you cannot do this alone. God's Word is a very important guide for forming your conscience. When you read, pray, and study Scripture, you strengthen your conscience.

Ways to Form Your Conscience

The Holy Spirit strengthens you to make good choices.

Prayer and study help you think things through.

Sacred Scripture and Church teaching guide your decisions.

Parents, teachers, and wise people give you advice.

Important Prayers

These are essential prayers that every Catholic should know. Latin is the official, universal language of the Church. No matter what language is someone's first or they speak daily, these prayers are prayed in common in Latin.

Sign of the Cross

In the name of the Father,
and of the Son,
and of the Holy Spirit.
Amen.

Signum Crucis

In nómine Patris
et Fílii
et Spíritus Sancti.
Amen.

The Lord's Prayer

Our Father, who art in heaven,
hallowed be thy name;
thy kingdom come,
thy will be done
on earth as it is in heaven.
Give us this day our daily bread,
and forgive us our trespasses,
as we forgive those who trespass
    against us;
and lead us not into temptation,
but deliver us from evil.

Pater Noster

Pater noster qui es in cælis:
santificétur Nomen Tuum;
advéniat Regnum Tuum;
fiat volúntas Tua,
sicut in cælo, et in terra.
Panem nostrum
cotidiánum da nobis hódie;
et dimítte nobis débita nostra,
sicut et nos
dimíttmus debitóribus nostris;
et ne nos indúcas in tentatiónem;
sed líbera nos a Malo.

The Hail Mary

Hail, Mary, full of grace,
the Lord is with thee.
Blessed art thou among women
and blessed is the fruit of thy womb,
   Jesus.
Holy Mary, Mother of God,
pray for us sinners,
now and at the hour of our death.
Amen.

Ave, Maria

Ave, María, grátia plena,
Dóminus tecum.
Benedícta tu in muliéribus,
et benedíctus fructus ventris
   tui, Iesus.
Sancta María, Mater Dei,
ora pro nobis peccatóribus,
nunc et in hora mortis nostræ.
Amen.

Glory Be

Glory be to the Father
and to the Son
and to the Holy Spirit,
as it was in the beginning
is now, and ever shall be
world without end.
Amen.

Gloria Patri

Gloria Patri
et Fílio
et Spíritui Sancto.
Sicut erat in princípio,
et nunc et semper
et in sæcula sæculorem.
Amen.

Prayers from the Sacraments

I Confess/*Confiteor*

I confess to almighty God
and to you, my brothers and sisters,
that I have greatly sinned,
in my thoughts and in my words,
in what I have done and in what I
have failed to do,

*Gently strike your chest with
a closed fist.*

through my fault, through my fault,
through my most grievous fault;

Continue:

therefore I ask blessed Mary
   ever-Virgin,
all the Angels and Saints,
and you, my brothers and sisters,
to pray for me to the Lord our God.

The Apostles' Creed

See page 304 for this prayer.

The Nicene Creed

See page 305 for this prayer.

Gloria

Glory to God in the highest,
and on earth peace to people of
   good will.

We praise you, we bless you, we adore
   you, we glorify you, we give you
   thanks for your great glory,
Lord God, heavenly King, O God,
   almighty Father.

Lord Jesus Christ,
Only Begotten Son,
Lord God, Lamb of God,
Son of the Father,
you take away the sins of the world,
have mercy on us;
you take away the sins of the world,
receive our prayer;
you are seated at the right hand of
the Father, have mercy on us.

For you alone are the Holy One,
you alone are the Lord,
you alone are the Most High,
Jesus Christ, with the Holy Spirit,
in the glory of God the Father.
Amen.

Holy, Holy, Holy Lord

Holy, Holy, Holy Lord God of hosts.
Heaven and earth are full of your glory.
Hosanna in the highest.
Blessed is he who comes in the name of the Lord.
Hosanna in the highest.

Act of Contrition

(From Rite of Penance)

Often used at night after a brief examination of conscience.

My God, I am sorry for my sins
with all my heart.
In choosing to do wrong
and failing to do good,
I have sinned against you
whom I should love above all things.
I firmly intend, with your help,
to do penance, to sin no more,
and to avoid whatever leads me to sin.
Our Savior Jesus Christ
suffered and died for us.
In his name, my God, have mercy.

The Jesus Prayer

Lord Jesus Christ, Son of God,
have mercy upon me, a sinner.

Personal and Family Prayers

Grace Before Meals

Bless us, O Lord, and these thy gifts
which we are about to receive
from thy bounty, through
Christ our Lord. Amen.

Grace After Meals

We give you thanks, Almighty God,
    for all your gifts
    which we have received,
    through Christ our Lord. Amen.

Angel Guardian

*An angel is a spiritual being that is a
messenger of God. Angels are mentioned
nearly 300 times in the Bible. Three
important angels are Gabriel, Michael,
and Raphael.*

Angel of God, my Guardian dear,
    to whom God's love commits me here.
Ever this day, be at my side,
    to light and guard, to rule and guide.
Amen.

Act of Faith, Hope, and Love

*Often prayed in the morning to remind us
that all gifts come from God, and that he
can help us believe, trust, and love.*

My God, I believe in you, I hope in
    you,
I love you above all things, with all
    my mind
and heart and strength.

Morning Prayer

Blessed are you, Lord, God of all
creation:
you take the sleep from my eyes
and the slumber from my eyelids.
Amen.

Evening Prayer

Protect us, Lord, as we stay awake;
watch over us as we sleep,
that awake, we may keep watch with
    Christ,
and asleep, rest in his peace.
Amen.

Bedtime Prayer

Dear God, as this day comes to
   an end,
bless my family and my friends.

Thank you for my happy day,
filled with laughter, learning,
   and play.

Stay with me while I sleep tonight,
and wake me with your morning light.

Good night, God.
Amen.

Birthday Blessing

Loving God,
you created all the people of the world
and you know each of us by name.
We thank you for N.,
who today celebrates his/her birthday.
Bless him/her with your love and friendship
that he/she may grow in wisdom, knowledge,
and grace.
May he/she love his/her family always
and be faithful to his/her friends.
Grant this through Christ our Lord.
Amen.

Praying with the Saints

When we pray with the Saints, we ask them to pray with us and for us. The Saints are with Christ. They speak for us when we need help.

A litany is a prayer with one line that is meant to be repeated so that those praying are caught up in the prayer itself. Some litanies are to Jesus; others are known as Litanies of the Saints.

Mary, Help of Those in Need

Holy Mary,
help those in need,
give strength to the weak,
comfort the sorrowful,
pray for God's people,
assist the clergy,
intercede for religious.
Mary, all who seek your help
experience your unfailing protection.
Amen.

Prayer for Saint Joseph's Day

Almighty God,
in your wisdom and love
you chose Joseph to be the husband
    of Mary, the mother of your Son.
As we enjoy his protection on earth
may we have the help of his prayers
    in Heaven.
We ask this through Christ our Lord.
Amen.

Litanies

Lord, have mercy.
Lord, have mercy.
Christ, have mercy.
Christ, have mercy.
Lord, have mercy.
Lord, have mercy.

Holy Mary, Mother of God,
pray for us
Saint John the Baptist, pray for us
Saint Joseph, pray for us
Saint Peter and Saint Paul,
pray for us

Lord [Jesus], we ask you,
hear our prayer.
Lord [Jesus], we ask you,
hear our prayer.

Christ, hear us.
Christ, graciously hear us.

Prayer for Saint Valentine's Day

God our Creator,
bless the love that brings people together
and grows ever stronger in our hearts.
May all the messages that carry the name
of your holy Bishop Valentine
be sent in good joy
and received in delight.
We ask this through Christ our Lord.
Amen.

Prayer of Saint Francis

Lord, make me an instrument of your peace;
where there is hatred, let me sow love;
where there is injury, pardon;
where there is doubt, faith;
where there is despair, hope;
where there is darkness, light;
and where there is sadness, joy.

Prayer of Petition

Lord God, you know our weakness.
In your mercy grant that the example
of your Saints may bring us back to
love and serve you through Christ
our Lord.
Amen.

Catholic Faith Words

A

absolution words spoken by the priest during the Sacrament of Penance and Reconciliation to grant forgiveness of sins in God's name (169)

angel a type of spiritual being that does God's work, such as delivering messages from God or helping to keep people safe from harm (98)

Apostles the Twelve disciples Jesus chose to be his closest followers. After the coming of the Holy Spirit, they shared in his work and mission in a special way. (111)

assembly the people gathered together for worship (225)

B

Baptism the Sacrament in which a person is immersed in water or has water poured on him or her. Baptism takes away Original Sin and all personal sin, and makes a person a child of God and member of the Church. (157)

Bible the Word of God written in human words. The Bible is the holy book of the Church. (75)

Blessed Sacrament a name for the Holy Eucharist, especially the Body of Christ kept in the Tabernacle (261)

blessing a prayer that blesses God, who is the source of everything that is good (212)

C

confession telling your sins to the priest (168)

conscience an ability given to us by God that helps us make choices about right and wrong (135)

consecration through the power of the Holy Spirit and the words and actions of the priest, the gifts of bread and wine become the Body and Blood of Jesus (247)

contrition being sorry for your sins and wanting to live better (167)

creation everything made by God (55)

creed a statement of the Church's beliefs (236)

D – F

disciples followers of Jesus who believe in him and live by his teachings (111)

Eucharist the Sacrament in which Jesus shares himself, and the bread and wine become his Body and Blood (225)

examination of conscience
a prayerful way of thinking about how we have followed the Ten Commandments, Beatitudes, and Church teachings (167)

faith believing in God and all that he helps us understand about himself. Faith leads us to obey God. (190)

free will being able to choose whether to obey God or disobey God. God created us with free will because he wants us to make good choices. (132)

G

God the Father the First Divine Person of the Holy Trinity (88)

Gospel a word that means "Good News." The Gospel message is the Good News of God's Kingdom and his saving love. (200)

grace God's gift of a share in his life and help (158)

Great Commandment the law to love God above all else and to love others the way you love yourself (123)

H – K

Heaven the full joy of living with God forever (278)

Holy Communion receiving Jesus' Body and Blood in the celebration of the Eucharist (258)

Holy Family the name for the human family of Jesus, Mary, and Joseph (100)

Holy Spirit the Third Divine Person of the Holy Trinity (108)

Holy Trinity the one God in three Divine Persons—God the Father, God the Son, and God the Holy Spirit (108)

homily a short talk about the readings at Mass (236)

intercession asking God to help others (212)

Kingdom of God the world of love, peace, and justice that is in Heaven and is still being built on Earth (192)

Last Supper the meal Jesus shared with his disciples on the night before he died. At the Last Supper, Jesus gave himself in the Eucharist. (244)

liturgy the public prayer of the Church. It includes the Sacraments and forms of daily prayer. (176)

Liturgy of the Eucharist the second main part of the Mass that includes Holy Communion (246)

Liturgy of the Word the first main part of the Mass during which we hear God's Word proclaimed (234)

Lord's Prayer the prayer that Jesus taught his disciples to pray to God the Father (210)

Mary the Mother of Jesus, the Mother of God. She is also called "Our Lady" because she is our Mother and the Mother of the Church. **(98)**

Mass the gathering of Catholics to worship God. It includes the Liturgy of the Word and the Liturgy of the Eucharist. **(225)**

mercy kindness and concern for those who are suffering. God has mercy on us even though we are sinners. **(143)**

mission a job or purpose. The Church's mission is to announce the Good News of God's Kingdom **(268)**

missionaries people who answer God's call to bring the message of Jesus and announce the Good News of his Kingdom to people in other places **(268)**

mortal sin a serious sin that causes a person's relationship with God to be broken **(135)**

New Commandment Jesus' command for his disciples to love one another as he has loved us **(124)**

New Testament the second part of the Bible about the life and teachings of Jesus, his followers, and the early Church **(77)**

Old Testament the first part of the Bible about God and his People before Jesus was born **(75)**

Original Sin the first sin committed by Adam and Eve and passed down to everyone **(65)**

parable a short story Jesus told about everyday life to teach something about God **(124)**

parish the local community of Catholics that meets at a particular place **(203)**

peace when things are calm and people get along with one another **(190)**

penance a prayer or an act to make up for sin **(168)**

Pentecost fifty days after the Resurrection when the Holy Spirit first came upon the Twelve disciples and the Church **(111)**

petition asking God for what we need **(212)**

praise giving God honor and thanks because he is God **(212)**

prayer talking to and listening to God **(91)**

Prayer of the Faithful prayer at Mass for the needs of the Church and the world **(236)**

proclaim to tell about Jesus in words and actions **(203)**

psalms poems and prayers from the Bible; they can be said or sung **(55)**

Real Presence the teaching that Jesus is really and truly with us in the Eucharist. We receive Jesus in his fullness. **(260)**

Resurrection the event of Jesus being raised from Death to new life by God the Father through the power of the Holy Spirit (179)

reverence the care and respect you show to God and holy persons and things (261)

Sacrament of Penance and Reconciliation the Sacrament in which God's forgiveness for sin is given through the Church (168)

sacramentals blessings, objects, and actions that remind you of God and are made sacred through the prayers of the Church (213)

Sacraments of Initiation the three Sacraments that celebrate membership in the Catholic Church: Baptism, Confirmation, and Eucharist (158)

sacrifice giving up something out of love for someone else or for the common good (good of everyone). Jesus sacrificed his life for all people. (244)

Saint a hero of the Church who loved God very much, led a holy life, and is now with God in Heaven (88)

Savior a title for Jesus, who was sent into the world to save all people lost through sin and to lead them back to God the Father (66)

Seven Sacraments special signs and celebrations that Jesus gave his Church. They allow us to share in God's life and work. (157)

sin a person's choice to disobey God on purpose and do what he or she knows is wrong. Accidents and mistakes are not sins. (56)

Son of God a name for Jesus that tells you God is his Father. The Son of God is the Second Divine Person of the Holy Trinity. (56)

Tabernacle the special place in the church where the Blessed Sacrament is reserved after Mass for those who are ill or for Eucharistic Adoration (261)

temptation wanting to do something we should not, or not doing something we should (143)

Ten Commandments God's laws that tell people how to love him and others (123)

thanksgiving giving thanks to God for all he has given us (212)

trust to believe in and depend on someone (91)

venial sin a sin that hurts a person's friendship with God, but does not completely break it (135)

virtues good habits that make you stronger and help you do what is right and good (143)

worship to adore and praise God, especially in the liturgy and in prayer (176)

Index

Boldfaced numbers refer to pages on which the terms are defined.

A

absolution **168**, 169, 314, 328
Act of Contrition 169, 170, 323
Act of Faith, Hope, and Love 324
Acts of the Apostles 79
Adam and Eve 52, 64, 65, 66, 142
Advent 19–24, 176, 178, 308
Advent wreath 23, 308
All Saints Day 16
Alphonsus Liguori, Saint 215
altar 225, 261, 313
angel 26, 27, 59, **98**, 99, 324, 328
Angel Guardian 324. *See also* Gabriel, Angel
Annunciation, the 99
Anointing of the Sick, Sacrament of the 159, 160, 307
Anthony Claret, Saint 273
Apostles 79, **111**, 112, 156, 179, 224, 258, 268, 269, 304, 306, 328
Apostles' Creed, the 240, 304, 322
"Appearance to the Disciples" 43
Arnold Janssen, Saint 113
Ascension 154, 245, 246, 306, 309, 310
Ash Wednesday 32, 309
assembly **225**, 226, 227, 228, 235, 236, 237, 246, 247, 248, 260, 262, 310, 328
Assumption of Mary 310

B

"Baptism of Jesus" 101
Baptism, Sacrament of 16, **157**, 158, 159, 160, 194, 225, 307, 328
Beatitudes 300, 315, 319
Bedtime Prayer 325
Benedict-Joseph Labré, Saint 171
Bible **4**, 5, 52, 54, 64, 65, 74, **75**, 77, 78, 79, 102, 168, 210, 214, 222, 235, 272, 281, 290, 292, 310, 324, 328. *See also* Sacred Scripture
Birthday Blessing 325
bishop(s) 160, 269, 273, 306
Blessed 12
    Imelda Lambertini 249
Blessed Sacrament **261**, 262, 328
blessing **212**, 213, 311, 316, 328
Body and Blood of Christ 159, 160, 222, 224, 246, 247, 249, 259, 260, 261, 310, 312, 313
Body of Christ (the Church) 157, 160, 304, 306

Book of Gospels 313
"The Boy Jesus in the Temple" 100
"The Bread of Life" 257
Brigid of Kildare, Saint 195

C

Call to Community 292–293
candles 313, 316
cantor 235
Care for Creation 302–303
Catholic Church 3, 4, 6, 10, 16, 26, 28, 32, 38, 39, 44, 86, 102, 111, 154, 157, 158, 159, 168, 178, 179, 193, 213, 222, 224, 227, 237, 260, 269, 271, 292, 293, 304, 305, 306, 307, 308, 309, 310, 312, 314, 316
    community 160, 292, 293
    forgiveness 165
    liturgy of the 176, 222
    member of the 16, 157, 158, 160, 193
    mission of the 268, 269, 271, 306
    teachings of the 237, 295, 296, 302, 315, 319
chalice 247, 261, 313
"Change Your Hearts" 19
charity 318. *See also* love
"Children of God" 1
choices 15, 21, 54, 64, 65, 68, 122, 134, 135, 136, 144, 146, 166, 167, 170, 319
Christ. *See* Jesus Christ
Christmas 10, 20, 25–30, 177, 308, 310
Church. *See* Catholic Church
Church year 10, 20, 44, 154, 175, 176, 177, 178, 179, 181, 306, 308
ciborium 313
"The Commissioning of the Apostles" 156
Communion 249, 311, 312
community 160, 224, 262, 292, 293
confession **168**, 169, 328
    individual 168, 314
Confirmation, Sacrament of 158, 159, 160, 307
conscience 120, **135**, 136, 167, 168, 314, 315, 319, 328. *See also* Examination of Conscience
consecration **246**, 247, 248, 310, 311, 328
contrition **167**, 314, 328
creation 54, **55**, 58, 328
creed **236**, 237, 304, 305, 311, 328
Cristóbal Magallanes Jara, Saint 69
Cross 11, 39, 170, 245, 248
    procession of 39, 41, 225, 226, 316

Cross, *continued*
    stations of the 309
    veneration of 309
crucifix 213, 316
cruets 313

D

David 38, 54, 55, 56, 63, 155
deacon(s) 157, 160, 203, 225, 228, 236, 261, 262, 268, 272
Dignity of Work, the 298–299
disciples 110, **111**, 328
disciples (the Twelve) 110, 111, 112, 179, 199, 297
discipleship 6, 10, 112, 159

E

Easter 10, 32, 38, 39, 43–46, 48, 177, 178, 179, 181, 304, 309, 310
Elizabeth (cousin of Mary) 11
Elizabeth of Hungary, Saint 127
Epistles 235, 239, 311
Eucharist, Sacrament of 3, 158, 159, 160, 161, 178, 222, 224, **225**, 228, 229, 246, 249, 256, 259, 261, 262, 263, 280, 307, 310, 311, 313, 328
Eucharistic Prayer 247, 248, 311
Evening Prayer 324
examination of conscience **167**, 315, 323, 329

F

faith 2, 6, 27, 77, 109, 147, **190**, 191, 304, 329
feast days 12, 26, 308
    of All Saints 16
    of Easter 178, 179
    of Mary 10
"The Feeding of Five Thousand" 258, 259
forgiveness 126, 133, 142, 144, 145, 146, 157, 166, 169, 247, 314
Frances Xavier Cabrini, Saint 270, 271
Francis, Pope 306
free will 64, 65, 68, **132**, 134, 136, 315, 329

G

Gabriel, Angel 59, 98, 99, 324
Garden of Eden 64
Gifts of the Holy Spirit 159, 160, 318
Gloria 27, 227, 311, 322

Glory Be 23, 213, 321
God 16, 56, 76, 158, 281, 319
  called by 16, 293, 303
  creation 55, 56, 58, 290, 294, 298, 300, 302, 303
  the Father. *See* God the Father
  forgiveness 3, 20, 120, 133, 160, 168, 171, 226, 227, 238, 281, 307, 314
  gifts from/of 52, 53, 54, 56, 58, 59, 98, 120, 135, 136, 191, 204, 280, 292, 302, 303, 315, 324
  grace of 16, 154, 160, 307, 315, 318
  the Holy Spirit. *See* Holy Spirit
  honor 227, 268, 307
  image and likeness 54, 55, 68, 291, 295
  laws of 122, 123, 135, 167, 234, 319
  love of/for 2, 3, 4, 16, 21, 32, 33, 52, 66, 74, 75, 76, 78, 86, 89, 92, 93, 102, 112, 120, 124, 126, 135, 156, 157, 158, 160, 177, 191, 193, 195, 202, 211, 234, 238, 248, 278, 280, 282, 293, 314, 315, 317, 318, 324
  mercy 2, 11, 20, 142, 314
  praising 2, 26, 54, 211, 227, 228, 247, 310
  promise of 63, 66
  relationship with 32, 75, 122, 126, 134, 135, 142, 167, 168, 212, 256, 259, 317
  respect for 211
  serving 160, 280, 307
  the Son. *See* Son of God, Jesus Christ
  trust in 86, 87, 90, 91, 92, 259, 324
  work of 270, 307
  worship 225
God the Father 44, 56, 57, 76, 78, 86, 87, **88**, 89, 90, 91, 109, 112, 120, 144, 156, 200, 202, 210, 237, 245, 278, 304, 329
Good Friday 38, 39, 179, 309
Good News 5, 16, 27, 48, 76, 156, 188, 199, 200, 203, 204, 236, 268, 269, 306
"Good Samaritan, The Parable of the" 124, 125, 126, 238
"The Good Shepherd" 67
Gospel **200**, 201, 202, 236, 268, 272, 329
Gospels, the (four) 5, 11, 77, 79, 236, 258, 313
grace 16, 154, **158**, 160, 315, 318, 329
Grace After Meals 324
Grace Before Meals 324

Great Amen 247
Great Commandment **123**, 126, 317, 329
"The Great Flood" 74

H

Hail Mary, the 13, 59, 213, 282, 321
Healing, Sacraments of 307
Heaven 16, 44, 48, 110, 188, 193, 256, **278**, 280, 283, 306, 323, 329
Hebrews 4, 19, 76, 122, 234
Holy Communion 160, 161, 222, 249, 256, **258**, 259, 260, 261, 262, 268, 272, 280, 281, 310, 311, 312, 329
Holy Days of Obligation 310
Holy Family **100**, 329
Holy, Holy, Holy Lord 323
Holy Orders, Sacrament of 159, 160, 307
Holy Saturday 38, 179
Holy Spirit 44, 48, 86, 101, 107, **108**, 109, 110, 111, 112, 113, 156, 158, 159, 167, 179, 202, 237, 247, 304, 329
  Fruits/Gifts of the 159, 160
  guidance of the 86, 110, 111, 135, 167, 202, 304, 319
  prayer for the 113, 114
Holy Thursday 38, 178
Holy Trinity 44, 86, **108**, 109, 156, 227, 237, 247, 304, 329
Holy Week 37, 38, 39, 40, 41
homily 228, **236**, 272, 329
hope 48, 318
human dignity 290, 298
Human Solidarity 300–301

I

I Confess/*Confiteor* 322
image and likeness 54, 55, 68, 291, 295
"Image of His Son" 15
Imelda Lambertini, Blessed 249
Immaculate Conception 308
Incarnation 154
Initiation, Sacraments of **158**, 159, 307, 331
intercession **212**, 329

J

Jane Frances de Chantal, Saint 147
Jesus Christ 20, 98, 110, 236, 244, 245, 258
  baptism of 26, 101, 308
  birth of 26, 79, 98, 99, 176, 177, 308

Jesus Christ, *continued*
  coming of 20, 308
  death of 38, 39, 170, 245, 246, 260
  divine and human 56, 57, 109
  forgiveness 126, 133, 142, 144, 145, 146
  God's gift 26, 52, 56
  life of 4, 5, 11, 44, 57, 78, 100, 101, 102, 176, 234, 247, 258, 297, 308
  love of/for 5, 133, 144, 156, 229, 238, 256, 259, 271
  miracles of 73, 155
  parables of **124**, 125, 126, 142, 143, 233, 234, 238, 278, 279, 330
  promise of 179, 201, 304
  relationship with 154, 228
  sacrifice of 3, 32, 160, 222, 243, 244, 245, 248, 259
  Second Coming 20, 194, 308
  the Savior 26, 32, 52, **66**, 67, 170, 179, 304, 331
  teachings of 4, 5, 10, 11, 16, 33, 63, 67, 76, 77, 78, 89, 91, 102, 109, 120, 123, 124, 126, 166, 188, 190, 191, 192, 194, 201, 202, 203, 210, 269, 270, 294, 296, 297, 300, 301
  works of 10, 32, 309
"Jesus Blesses the Children" 192
"Jesus Heals a Blind Man" 155
Jesus Prayer, the 323
"Jesus' Disciples Receive a Mission" 199
Jewish faith and customs 56, 76
John Bosco, Saint 88, 89
John the Baptist 4, 19, 101, 308
Joseph, husband of Mary 56, 100, 326
Julian of Norwich 93
justice 188, 192, 211, 234

K

Kingdom of God 5, 188, 189, **192**, 193, 194, 203, 205, 234, 256, 268, 269, 306, 329
Kyrie 226, 331

L

Lamb of God 256, 259, 311
Last Supper, the 178, **244**, 245, 247, 260, 329
Lectern 313
lectionary 313
Lent 31–36, 38, 178, 309
Leo XIII, Pope 270
"Let the Children Come" 189
letters of the New Testament. *See* Epistles

Index

Life and Dignity 290–291
litany 316, 326
liturgy **176**, 329
Liturgy of the Eucharist 222, **246**, 310, 311, 329
Liturgy of the Word 222, **234**, 235, 310, 311, 329
Lord's Prayer, the 45, 188, 209, **210**, 211, 214, 216, 259, 311, 314, 320, 329
"Lost Sheep, Parable of the" 238
love 11, 89, 92, 120, 123, 126, 132, 144, 147, 160, 188, 193, 244, 246, 260, 300
    your neighbor 33, 102, 124, 125, 126, 127, 238, 281, 292, 294, 296, 300, 301
Luke, Saint 79

M

Mary 4, 9, 10, 56, 59, 79, **98**, 99, 100, 179, 299, 306, 308, 316, 326, 330. *See also* Rosary, Hail Mary
    forgiveness 10, 11
    love of/for 10, 11
    Mother of God 10, 59, 282, 306, 316
    Mother of the Church 59
    Our Lady of Mercy 10
Mary Magdalena de Pazzi, Saint 283
Mass 3, 4, 27, 54, 69, 77, 122, 181, 193, 222, **225**, 227, 228, 229, 235, 239, 245, 246, 248, 249, 259, 261, 262, 268, 272, 280, 281, 304, 305, 307, 310, 312, 313, 315, 330
    Order of 311
Matrimony, Sacrament of 159, 160, 307
mercy 142, **143**, 148, 330
Michael, Angel 324
mission 16, 256, **268**, 269, 330
    of the Church 268, 269, 271, 306
missionaries **268**, 269, 270, 330
Missionaries of Charity 205
Morning Prayer 324
mortal sin **135**, 330
Moses 121, 122
Mother Teresa 205
"Mustard Seed, The Parable of the" 234
Mystery of Faith, the 247, 248, 311

N

New Commandment 120, **124**, 125, 126, 318, 330
New Testament 4, 5, **77**, 235, 311, 313, 330

Nicene Creed, the 305, 322
Noah 74, 75

O

obedience 56, 65, 100, 122, 134, 143, 167, 281, 315, 317
Old Testament 4, **75**, 77, 235, 311, 330
Option for the Poor 296–297
Order of Mass 311
Ordinary Time 9–18, 177, 309
Original Sin 64, **65**, 330

P

parable **124**, 234, 238, 330. *See also individual parables*
parish **203**, 330
Passion (Palm) Sunday 38, 309
paten 313
"Paul Proclaims the Kingdom" 267
Paul, Saint 79, 239, 267
peace 160, 188, **190**, 191, 193, 211, 234, 300, 330
penance **168**, 169, 314, 330
Penance and Reconciliation, Sacrament of 3, 123, 133, 144, 159, 160, **168**, 169, 170, 281, 307, 314, 315, 331
Pentecost 47–50, 110, **111**, 179, 309, 330
People of God 54, 75, 76, 293, 306
Peter, Saint 103, 131, 132, 133, 141, 268, 269, 306
petition **212**, 330
Pierre Toussaint, Venerable 263
Pius X, Saint 161
Pope 103, 161, 181, 269, 306
    Francis 306
    Leo XIII 270
    Pius IX 161
praise **212**, 259, 330
prayer 2, 6, **91**, 93, 126, 209, 210, 212, 213, 227, 234, 316, 330
    of blessing 60, 182, **212**, 274
    daily 324
    of intercession 40, 94, **212**
    of petition 22, 128, 138, 148, 172, **212**, 264, 327
    of praise 28, 70, 128, **212**, 215, 230
    signing 34, 104
    of thanksgiving 17, 28, 206, **212**, 310
Prayer of the Faithful 40, **236**, 237, 311, 330
priest(s) 157, 160, 168, 169, 170, 203, 225, 226, 227, 228, 236, 246, 247, 248, 260, 261, 262, 268, 272

procession with the Cross 39, 41, 225, 226
proclaim 202, **203**, 330
"Prodigal Son, Parable of the" 142, 143, 238
promise 63, 66, 170, 171, 179
psalms 54, **55**, 77, 214, 235, 330

R

Raphael, Angel 324
Real Presence 256, **260**, 261, 262, 310, 330
Resurrection 44, 154, **179**, 245, 246, 247, 248, 309, 331
reverence **261**, 307, 312, 331
"Rich Young Man, The Parable of the" 244
Rights and Responsibilities 294–295
"Risen Jesus Appears to the Disciples" 107
"The Road to Emmaus" 223
Roman Missal, the 313
Rosary, the 304, 316
Rose of Lima, Saint 296

S

sacramentals **213**, 316, 331
Sacred Scripture 4, 75, 234, 296, 298, 314, 319. *See also* Bible
sacrifice 160, 222, **244**, 245, 259, 331
Saint 10, 12, 16, **88**, 271, 306, 308, 326, 331
    Alphonsus Liguori 215
    Anthony Claret 273
    Arnold Janssen 113
    Benedict-Joseph Labré 171
    Brigid of Kildare 195
    Cristóbal Magallanes Jara 69
    Elizabeth of Hungary 127
    Frances Xavier Cabrini 270, 271
    Jane Frances de Chantal 147
    John Bosco 88, 89
    Luke 79
    Mary Magdalena de Pazzi 283
    Paul 79, 239
    Peter 103, 131, 132, 133, 141, 268, 269
    Pius X 161
    Rose of Lima 296
    Tarcisius 229
    Teresa of Calcutta 205
    Thérèse of Lisieux 137
    Victor 181
Saint Francis, Prayer of 327
Saint Joseph's Day, prayer for 326
Saint Valentine's Day, prayer for 327
Sarto, Giuseppe (Pope Pius X) 161
Savior 26, 32, 52, **66**, 67, 98, 99, 170, 179, 248, 304, 331

Service of Communion, Sacraments at the 307
Seven Sacraments **3**, 154, 155, **157**, 158, 272, 307, 331
  Anointing of the Sick 159, 160, 307
  Baptism 16, **157**, 158, 159, 160, 162, 225, 307, 328
  Confirmation 158, 159, 160, 307
  Eucharist 3, 158, 159, 160, 161, 178, 222, 224, 225, 228, 229, 246, 249, 256, 259, 261, 262, 263, 280, 307, 310, 311, 313, 328
  Holy Orders 159, 160, 307
  Matrimony 159, 160, 307
  Penance and Reconciliation 3, 123, 144, 159, 160, **168**, 169, 170, 281, 307, 314, 315, 331
sign of peace 260, 311, 316
Sign of the Cross 34, 109, 169, 213, 225, 226, 316, 320
"Signing of the Senses" 35
sin 11, 32, **56**, 134, 142, 160, 166, 211, 260, 314, 315, 331
  mortal **135**
  power of 170, 245
  saved from 39
  venial **135**
"The Sinner Who Repents" 63
Solemnity of Mary, Mother of God 310

Solemnity of the Immaculate Conception 310
Son of God 2, 52, **56**, 57, 86, 97, 99, 100, 103, 109, 177, 202, 237, 304, 308, 331

Tabernacle **261**, 262, 313, 331
Tarcisius, Saint 229
temptation 142, **143**, 331
Ten Commandments 121, 122, **123**, 135, 167, 315, 317, 331
Teresa of Calcutta, Saint 205
thanksgiving **212**, 331
Theological Virtues 318. *See also* faith, hope, charity (love)
Thérèse of Lisieux, Saint 137
Triduum 37–42, 309
Trinity. *See* Holy Trinity
trust **91**, 92, 331

Venerable 12
  Pierre Toussaint 263
venial sin **135**, 331
Victor, Saint 181
"The Vine and the Branches" 201
virtues 142, **143**, 318, 331
  Theological 318

"The Wedding at Cana" 9
"The Wedding Feast" 278, 279
"Whose Sins You Forgive" 165
"The Woman Who Was Forgiven" 166
Word of God 4, 75, 77, 111, 222, 235, 281, 310, 313, 319
work
  dignity of 298
  value of 299
worship 78, **176**, 224, 225, 307, 310, 331

"Yeast, The Parable of the" 233

Zacchaeus 190, 191, 193

Photo Credits

v © Our Sunday Visitor; **vii** © Our Sunday Visitor; **viii** Our Sunday Visitor; **1** © Stockbyte/Thinkstock; **2** © iStockphoto.com/Mike Sonnenberg; **3** © Bill & Peggy Wittman; **5** © iStockphoto.com/Skip ODonnell; **6** © Ocean/Corbis; **7** (bg) © Image Copyright Joan Kerrigan, 2012 Used under license from Shutterstock.com; **7** (inset) © Image Copyright Zvonimir Orec, 2012 Used under license from Shutterstock.com; **10** Hemera/Thinkstock; **11** © Digital Vision/Thinkstock; **13** Image Copyright Philip Meyer, 2012 Used under license from Shutterstock.com; **14** (t) © Alan Spence/age fotostock; **14** (b) © Digital Vision/Thinkstock; **15** © Bill & Peggy Wittman; **16** © Bill & Peggy Wittman; **17** © Image Copyright Philip Meyer, 2012 Used under license from Shutterstock.com; **18** (t) © Robert Harding Picture Library Ltd/Alamy; **18** (b) © Bill & Peggy Wittman; **20** © David Young-Wolff/PhotoEdit; **22–23** © Image Copyright Philip Meyer, 2012 Used under license from Shutterstock.com; **24** (t) © David Young-Wolff/PhotoEdit; **24** (b) © Thomas Northcut/Photodisc/Thinkstock; **25** © Photo by Janet Jensen/Tacoma News Tribune/MCT via Getty Images; **26** © Image Copyright djem, 2012 Used under license from Shutterstock.com; **28–29** (bg) © Image Copyright Philip Meyer, 2012 Used under license from Shutterstock.com; **30** © Image Copyright Artisticco, 2012 Used under license from Shutterstock.com; **31** © Image Copyright CREATISTA, 2012 Used under license from Shutterstock.com; **32** © M.T.M. Images/Alamy; **33** © Bill & Peggy Wittman; **34–35** (bg) © Image Copyright Philip Meyer, 2012 Used under license from Shutterstock.com; **36** (t) © Universal Images Group/DeAgostini/Alamy; **36** (b) © Bill & Peggy Wittman; **38** © Bill & Peggy Wittman; **40–41** (bg) © Image Copyright Philip Meyer, 2012 Used under license from Shutterstock.com; **42** © Stockbyte/Thinkstock; **43** © Stockbyte/Thinkstock; **44** © iStockphoto/Thinkstock; **45** (bg) © Image Copyright Philip Meyer, 2012 Used under license from Shutterstock.com; **46** (t) © Image Copyright Keith McIntyre, 2012 Used under license from Shutterstock.com; **46** (b) © Stockbyte/Thinkstock; **49** (bg) © Image Copyright Philip Meyer, 2012 Used under license from Shutterstock.com; **50** © Image Copyright Bocman1973, 2012 Used under license from Shutterstock.com; **52** (t) © Our Sunday Visitor; **52** (b) © PhotoAlto/Laurence Mouton/Getty Images; **53** © iStockphoto.com/Jani Bryson; **54** (br) © Kayte Deioma/PhotoEdit; **54** (bc) Superstock; **54–55** (bg) © iStockphoto.com/Robert Churchill; **56** © Carlos's Pemium Images/Alamy; **57** © SuperStock/Glowimages; **58** © Carlos's Pemium Images/Alamy; **60** (bg) © Image Copyright Joan Kerrigan, 2012 Used under license from Shutterstock.com; **60** (inset) © iStockphoto/Thinkstock; **61** © SuperStock/Glowimages; **63** © iStockphoto.com/Shawn Gearhart; **64** © IMAGEZOO/SuperStock; **68** © Tuan Tran/Flickr/Getty Images; **69** (l) © Photos.com/Thinkstock; **69** (c) © Brand X Pictures/Thinkstock; **69** (r) © iStockphoto.com/Jaren Wicklund; **70** (bg) © Image Copyright Joan Kerrigan, 2012 Used under license from Shutterstock.com; **70** (inset) © Godong/Robert Harding World Imagery/Getty Images; **71** © iStockphoto.com/Shawn Gearhart; **76** © Image Copyright magicinfoto, 2012 Used under license from Shutterstock.com; **77** © iStockphoto.com/Nicole S. Young; **78** © Digital Vision/Thinkstock; **80** (bg) © Image Copyright Joan Kerrigan, 2012 Used under license from Shutterstock.com; **80** (inset) © iStockphoto.com/Jason Doiy; **81** © iStockphoto.com/Nicole S. Young; **86** (t) © iStockphoto.com/Andrew Howe; **86** (b) © Our Sunday Visitor; **87** © iStockphoto/Thinkstock; **88** © Exactostock/SuperStock; **90** © iStockphoto/Thinkstock; **91** © The Crosiers/Gene Plaisted, OSC; **94** (bg) © Image Copyright Joan Kerrigan, 2012 Used under license from Shutterstock.com; **94** (inset) © SuperStock/Ken Seet/Corbis; **95** © The Crosiers/Gene Plaisted, OSC; **97** (l) © iStockphoto/Thinkstock; **97** (r) © Image Copyright Sergii Figurny, 2012 Used under license from Shutterstock.com; **98** (l) © Image Copyright Zvonimir Atletic, 2012 Used under license from Shutterstock.com; **98** (r) © Image Copyright Zvonimir Atletic, 2012 Used under license from Shutterstock.com; **98** (inset) © iStockphoto/Thinkstock; **101** © Sean Justice/Corbis; **102** © JGI/Jamie Grill/Blend Images/Corbis; **104** (bg) © Image Copyright Joan Kerrigan, 2012 Used under license from Shutterstock.com; **104** (inset) © PhotoSpin/age fotostock; **107** © iStockphoto.com/Hallgerd; **109** © iStockphoto.com/Jaren Wicklund; **112** © iStockphoto/Thinkstock; **113** © Ingram Publishing/Thinkstock; **114** (bg) © Image Copyright Joan Kerrigan, 2012 Used under license from Shutterstock.com; **114** (inset) © FogStock LLC/SuperStock; **120** (c) © iStockphoto/Thinkstock; **120** (b) © The Crosiers/Gene Plaisted; **121** © iStockphoto.com/Patrick Herrera; **126** © Stockbyte/Thinkstock; **128** (bg) © Image Copyright Joan Kerrigan, 2012 Used under license from Shutterstock.com; **128** (inset) © Image Copyright Zvonimir Atletic, 2012 Used under license from Shutterstock.com; **129** © iStockphoto.com/Patrick Herrera; **132** © Photoservice Electa/Universal Images Group/Getty Images; **133** (t) © Feed My Lambs, illustration for 'The Life of Christ', c.1884–96 (w/c & gouache on paperboard), Tissot, James Jacques Joseph (1836–1902)/Brooklyn Museum of Art, New York, USA/Bridgeman Images; **133** (b) © Myrleen Pearson; **134** (l) © Image Copyright Ilike, 2012 Used under license from Shutterstock.com; **134** (r) © Somos Images/age fotostock; **138** (bg) © Image Copyright Joan Kerrigan, 2012 Used under license from Shutterstock.com; **138** (inset) © Photos.com/Thinkstock; **141** (c) © Fancy Collection/SuperStock; **146** © Odilon Dimier/PhotoAlto/Corbis; **148** (bg) © Image Copyright Joan Kerrigan, 2012 Used under license from Shutterstock.com; **148** (inset) © Our Sunday Visitor; **149** © Fancy Collection/SuperStock; **154** (c) © Bill & Peggy Wittman; **154** (b) © Jim West/age fotostock; **155** (b) © Image Copyright Valua Vitaly, 2012 Used under license from Shutterstock.com; **156** (t) © Photo by Alinari/Alinari Archives, Florence/Alinari via Getty Images; **156** (b) © Ryan McVay/Photodisc/Thinkstock; **157** © David Young-Wolff/PhotoEdit; **159** (t) © Bill & Peggy Wittman; **162** (bg) © Image Copyright Joan Kerrigan, 2012 Used under license from Shutterstock.com; **162** (inset) © Design Pics Inc./Alamy; **163** © David Young-Wolff/PhotoEdit; **166** © zatletic/Bigstock.com; **169** (t) © Our Sunday Visitor; **169** (c) © Our Sunday Visitor; **169** (b) © Our Sunday Visitor; **172** (bg) © Image Copyright Joan Kerrigan, 2012 Used under license from Shutterstock.com; **172** (inset) © Image Copyright Zack Clothier, 2012 Used under license from Shutterstock.com; **173** © Our Sunday Visitor; **175** © david sanger photography/Alamy; **176–177** (bg) © Adrian Sherratt/Alamy; **176** (inset) © iStockphoto/Thinkstock; **177** (c) © iStockphoto/Thinkstock; **178** © Jim West/Alamy; **182** (bg) © Image Copyright Joan Kerrigan, 2012 Used under license from Shutterstock.com; **182** (inset) © laurentiu iordache/Alamy; **183** © iStockphoto/Thinkstock; **188** (t) © Bill & Peggy Wittman; **188** (b) © Photo by Joe Raedle/Getty Images; **189** (bg) © Image Copyright Frannyanne, 2012 Used under license from Shutterstock.com; **189** (l) © Our Sunday Visitor;

189 (r) © Our Sunday Visitor; **192** © Comstock/Thinkstock; **193** (t) © Image Copyright Maria Dryfhout, 2012 Used under license from Shutterstock.com; **193** (b) © Our Sunday Visitor; **196** (bg) © Image Copyright Joan Kerrigan, 2012 Used under license from Shutterstock.com; **196** (inset) © Image Copyright Kaetana, 2012 Used under license from Shutterstock.com; **197** © Comstock/Thinkstock; **199** © iStockphoto.com/Pathathai Chungyam; **200** © Jim West/age fotostock; **202** (tl) © P Deliss/GODONG; **202** (cr) © Blend Images/SuperStock; **202** (bl) © Our Sunday Visitor; **203** (l) © Mario Ponta/age fotostock; **203** (r) © Our Sunday Visitor; **206** (bg) © Image Copyright Joan Kerrigan, 2012 Used under license from Shutterstock.com; **206** (inset) © Creatas/Thinkstock; **207** © Jim West/age fotostock; **209** © Our Sunday Visitor; **210** © Christie's Images Ltd./SuperStock; **211** © Image Copyright Zurijeta, 2012 Used under license from Shutterstock.com; **215** © iStockphoto.com/Maria Pavlova; **216** (bg) © Image Copyright Joan Kerrigan, 2012 Used under license from Shutterstock.com; **216** (inset) © mandy godbehear/Bigstock.com; **217** © Our Sunday Visitor; **222** (t) © Our Sunday Visitor; **222** (b) © Corbis/SuperStock; **225** © Our Sunday Visitor; **226** © Our Sunday Visitor; **227** © Our Sunday Visitor; **228** (t) © Bill & Peggy Wittman; **228** (b) © age fotostock/robertharding/Godong; **230** (bg) © Image Copyright Joan Kerrigan, 2012 Used under license from Shutterstock.com; **230** (inset) © Our Sunday Visitor; **231** © age fotostock/robertharding/Godong; **233** © iStockphoto.com/eggeegjiew; **235** © Our Sunday Visitor; **236** © Our Sunday Visitor; **237** © Bill & Peggy Wittman; **239** © Kayte Deioma/PhotoEdit; **240** (bg) © Image Copyright Joan Kerrigan, 2012 Used under license from Shutterstock.com; **240** (inset) © Bill & Peggy Wittman; **241** © Our Sunday Visitor; **243** © iStockphoto.com/dtimiraos; **245** (t) © Image Copyright Zvonimir Atletic, Used under license from Shutterstock.com; **245** (b) © Myrleen Pearson; **246** © Bill & Peggy Wittman; **247** © Our Sunday Visitor; **248** © Image Copyright Sergii Figurny, 2012 Used under license from Shutterstock.com; **250** (bg) © Image Copyright Joan Kerrigan, 2012 Used under license from Shutterstock.com; **250** (inset) © Robert Harding Picture Library/age fotostock; **251** © Our Sunday Visitor; **256** (t) © Peter Mather/First Light/Getty Images; **256** (b) © iStockphoto.com/g01xm; **257** © Our Sunday Visitor; **260** © Our Sunday Visitor; **261** © Our Sunday Visitor; **262** © Our Sunday Visitor; **264** © Image Copyright Joan Kerrigan, 2012 Used under license from Shutterstock.com; **264** (inset) © David Young-Wolff/PhotoEdit; **265** © Our Sunday Visitor; **268** © Our Sunday Visitor; **269** © Joseph Project-Malawi/Alamy; **270** (l) © Folio/Alamy; **270** (r) © iStockphoto.com/Kim Gunkel; **270** (inset) © iStockphoto/Thinkstock; **274** (bg) © Image Copyright Joan Kerrigan, 2012 Used under license from Shutterstock.com; **275** © iStockphoto.com/Kim Gunkel; **277** © Our Sunday Visitor; **280** © iStockphoto.com/Glenda Powers; **281** (t) © Bill & Peggy Wittman; **281** (b) © iStockphoto/Thinkstock; **280** © Our Sunday Visitor; **284** © iStockphoto.com/Magdalena Kucova; **284** (bg) © Image Copyright Joan Kerrigan, 2012 Used under license from Shutterstock.com; **285** © iStockphoto.com/Glenda Powers; **290** (cl) © iStockphoto.com/blackred; **290–291** (cr) © iStockphoto.com/blackred; **290** (bl) © Ariel Skelley/Blend Images/Getty; **290–291** (br) © iStockphoto.com/blackred; **291** (tr) © iStockphoto.com/blackred; **291** (cr) © iStockphoto.com/blackred; **292** (l) © Dennis MacDonald/Alamy; **292** (r) © iStockphoto.com/kickstand; **294** © iStockphoto.com/Steve Debenport; **296** © Ton Koene/age fotostock; **298** © PhotoAlto/SuperStock; **299** © iStockphoto.com/Blend_Images; **300** © Tim Gainey/Alamy; **302** © John Lund/Sam Diephui/age fotostock; **305** © The Crosiers/Gene Plaisted, OSC; **306** © FILIPPO MONTEFORTE,FILIPPO MONTEFORTE/AFP/Getty Images; **312** © Jim West/Alamy; **314** © Our Sunday Visitor; **316** (t) © Our Sunday Visitor; **316** (b) © Stockbyte/Thinkstock; **317** (t) © Our Sunday Visitor; **319** © Our Sunday Visitor

Acknowledgements:

For permission to reprint copyrighted material, grateful acknowledgment is made to the following sources:

International Consultation on English Texts: English translation of Glory Be (the *Gloria Patri*), Lord, have mercy, Apostles' Creed, Nicene Creed, the Lord's Prayer, and Lamb of God (*Agnus Dei*) by the International Consultation on English Texts (ICET). All rights reserved.

The English translation of the Confiteor, Order of Mass, Holy, Holy, Holy, Lord (*the Sanctus*), and Angel Guardian from *The Roman Missal* © 2010, International Commission on English in the Liturgy Corporation (ICEL): All rights reserved.

The English translation of the Act of Contrition from the *Rite of Penance* © 1974, ICEL: English translation. All rights reserved.

"Bedtime Prayer" from *My Book of Prayers* © 2010, Our Sunday Visitor, Inc. All rights reserved.

The Liturgical Conference: Adapted from "February 14, St. Valentine's Day" (Retitled: "Prayer for St. Valentine's Day") in *Major Feasts and Seasons*.

Liturgy Training Publications, 1800 North Hermitage Avenue, Chicago Il 60622, 1-800-933-1800, www.ltp.org: From "Meal Prayer for Harvest Time" (Retitled: "Grace Before Mealtime") in *Blessings and Prayer through the Year: A Resource for School and Parish* by Elizabeth McMahon Jeep. Text © 2004 by Archdiocese of Chicago.

Twenty-Third Publications, A Division of Bayard: "Grace After Meals" (Retitled: "Grace After Mealtime") from *500 Prayers for Catholic Schools and Parish Youth Groups* by Filomena Tassi and Peter Tassi. Text copyright © Filomena Tassi and Peter Tassi.

United States Conference of Catholic Bishops, Inc., Washington, D.C.: "At Bedside" (Retitled: "Evening Prayer") and "Washing and Dressing" (Retitled: "Morning Prayer") from *Catholic Household Blessings and Prayers*. Translation copyright © 1989 by United States Catholic Conference, Inc. From English translation of "Blessing on Birthdays or the Anniversary of Baptism" (Retitled: "Birthday Blessing") in *Book of Blessings*. Translation copyright © 1988 by United States Catholic Conference, Inc.